CARLSBAD UNION SCHOOL DISTRICT

ISSUED TO:	DATE:

AMERICA'S

OWN STORY

AMERICA'S

OWN STORY

by

VANZA DEVEREAUX

Illustrated by

WARREN CHASE MERRITT

CALIFORNIA STATE SERIES
PUBLISHED BY
CALIFORNIA STATE DEPARTMENT OF EDUCATION
SACRAMENTO, 1956

printed in
CALIFORNIA STATE PRINTING OFFICE
SACRAMENTO 2ND PRINT, 50M 1957

PUBLISHER'S FOREWORD

America's Own Story is dedicated to the preservation of the *American way of life*.

There are those who seek to destroy this way of life. We who believe in it must protect it. One of our greatest protections is a sound understanding of what America really means.

Our children must learn early in life what the American way *is* — and how it came to be. They must learn not to take for granted the rights of "life, liberty, and the pursuit of happiness." They must understand, and value, our great heritage if they are to preserve it.

America's Own Story is a social studies text that aims at a fuller appreciation of, and participation in, a *living America*. It is not only for "citizens-to-be," but for "citizens-who-are" — the boys and girls who attend America's schools.

CONTENTS

Part II   OUR COUNTRY BEGINS

CONTENTS

Part III   THE NATION MOVES WESTWARD

Story One

Story Two

Story Three

Part IV   OUR COUNTRY GROWS UP

Part I—A NEW WORLD IS FOUND

Before You Read the Story——

Many, many years ago there was not a country called the United States. There were not even white men living here. The land belonged to the Indians.

For hundreds of years the Indians lived here alone. They roamed over the great plains and through the wide valleys. They paddled their canoes upon the lakes and rivers. They were happy and contented. They did not dream that there were white men in the world!

Neither did the white men in Europe dream that there were Indians in a land across the sea. They did not know that to the west was a great New World.

What happened? How did the white men learn that there were Indians in America? How did they discover the New World? How did the United States become the country that it is today?

It is a strange and interesting story. It is like a puzzle with many pieces that fit together. Two of the pieces in the puzzle are a *book* and a *voyage*. Could a book and a voyage help to discover America? They did!

The book made men want to discover new and strange lands. The voyage proved to them that the world is round. This story will tell you about the book that helped discover America. The next story will tell you about the voyage.

After you have read this story, discuss with your classmates how the *book* made men want to discover new lands. Discuss how it gave them new ideas about their ways of living. Discuss how the book might have helped Europeans discover America.

THE OLD WORLD
SEEKS THE NEW

AMERICA IS FOUND AND LOST AGAIN

In northern Europe are the countries of Denmark, Sweden, and Norway. A thousand years ago the people in these countries were called Northmen. The Northmen were a warlike and adventurous people. The men built long, narrow ships and sailed far out upon the sea. They often plundered distant cities they visited. They robbed other ships at sea. Before long they came to be known as Vikings. The word *viking* means sea rover, or pirate.

Vikings from Norway discovered the islands of Iceland and Greenland. They built homes there, but the men still loved the sea. Leif Ericson, or Leif the Lucky, took a party of men and sailed still farther to the west. He found a beautiful new land covered with tall trees, dense vegetation, and wild grapevines.

The grapevines gave Leif an idea. "I will name this new land *Vineland*, or *Vinland*," he said. Vinland was on the northeastern coast of North America.

Northmen from Greenland went to Vinland to live. But they quarreled with the natives. They even quarreled among themselves. Finally they sailed back to Greenland.

The Northmen discovered America nearly one thousand years ago, but *they did not return there. They did not tell anyone about their discovery.* America was found and lost again!

3

The Vikings were bold and daring seamen. They sailed their long, narrow ships far to the west in search of new adventure.

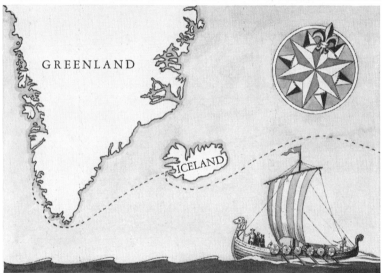

GREENLAND

ICELAND

The Vikings landed on the coasts of Iceland and Greenland. They began colonies on the barren shores of the rocky islands.

But they still loved the sea. Through storms and fields of icebergs, Leif Ericson and his men sailed still farther west.

4

Finally they came to a new land on the coast of North America. Leif Ericson named the new land Vineland, or Vinland.

The Vikings who settled there did not get along well with the natives. They quarreled with each other. Finally they returned home.

They did not tell anyone of their discovery. Thus the New World — the land we call America — was found and lost again.

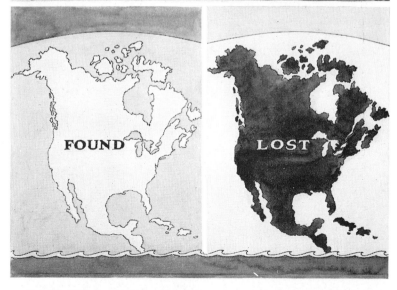

FOUND

LOST

Marco Polo was born in Venice, Italy, many years ago. His father and his uncle were merchant traders. When Marco was seventeen, they took him with them to China and the Far East. At that time China was a very rich and prosperous country. Marco saw many things he had not seen in Europe. He saw beautiful buildings, lovely silks, precious jewels, and costly treasures.

His father and uncle had seen the wonders of China many years before, but the sights were all new and interesting to Marco. He liked to watch the silkworms as they spun the dainty thread that was made into beautiful cloth. He liked to eat from the thin china dishes and to look at the beautiful pictures painted by the Chinese artists. He was interested in the Chinese water clocks and the paper money that was used in trade.

But perhaps the two things that interested Marco most were the Chinese system of waterways and the Great Wall of China. Even in those early times the Chinese had built waterways throughout their country. Canals had been dug from one river to another so that the water flowed in long, continuous waterways. The Chinese people could travel thousands of miles through their country in boats.

The Great Wall of China was built to keep out warring tribes that roamed over the plains of Asia. The wall was about twenty feet thick and thirty feet high. It stretched along the border of China for fifteen hundred miles and protected the Chinese from unfriendly neighbors.

Marco, his father, and his uncle were received at the court of the Chinese Emperor, Kublai Khan. The Emperor liked Marco very much and gave him important work to do. As Marco traveled about China, and even to other countries, he kept careful notes so that he could report to the Emperor when he returned.

For a time the Polos were very happy in China. Then they grew restless and wanted to return to their old home in Venice. The Emperor did not want them to go, but he finally gave his consent.

It took Marco, his father, and his uncle three years to make the journey home. When they reached Venice they were tired and dirty. Their clothes were old and ragged. They told the people of the wonderful things they had seen in China and the Far East, but no one would believe them.

The travelers decided to invite some of their friends and relatives to a banquet. During the banquet the Polos wore beautiful clothes, but after the banquet they put on the ragged clothes they had worn when they returned to Venice. They ripped open the seams of their old clothes. Emeralds, rubies, diamonds, pearls, and other precious jewels rolled out. The people stared at the costly jewels.

"Your stories must be true!" they exclaimed. They welcomed the three men back to their old home.

Some time later Marco became a soldier and fought for Venice. During the war he was captured and put into prison. Marco Polo had *told* people about his adventures, but he had never *written* about them. While he was in prison he told the story of his adventures to a writer. The writer made the stories into a book.

The book told about Marco Polo's adventures in China and the Far East. It told about the beautiful treasures from the East. It also said that China and India were bounded on the east by an ocean. Men began to wonder. Could this be the same ocean that bounded Europe on the west? If it *were* the same ocean, could men sail *west*, go around the world, and reach China?

Marco Polo, his father, and his uncle went to China. In China they saw riches, spices, and beautiful silks not known in Europe.

They went to the court of the Emperor Kublai Khan. The Emperor liked Marco and gave him very important positions.

The Polos returned to Venice. The people did not believe the stories of the East until the Polos displayed their jewels.

The people of
Europe wanted
the treasures
from the East.
But the only
route was over
hot, sandy des-
erts and high
mountains.

Marco Polo
wrote a book
that told of
the wonders of
the East. He
also told of
an ocean that
touched China
on the east.

People began
to wonder. Was
there a new
route to the
East? Could
men find a
waterway that
would be safer
and shorter?

9

For many years the people of Europe had lived much as their fathers had lived. But little by little their ways of living began to change. People read the stories of Marco Polo's adventures. They heard stories told by other travelers.

Some of the travelers brought back the precious things from the East. They brought back spices, perfumes, lovely silks, soft rugs, and precious jewels. The people of Europe had not known these things. Their food was coarse and often spoiled. Their clothes were plain and ugly. Their homes were bare, their furniture hard and uncomfortable.

The spices and pepper from the East made their food taste better. The colorful silks made beautiful garments. The rugs from the East made soft coverings. The fine woods made beautiful furniture.

"You must travel to the distant lands," the people told the traders of that day. "You must bring back the wonderful things from the East."

In those days ships could not travel all the way to the Far East. They could travel only as far as Turkey. From there the goods had to be carried many miles on the backs of camels. This was a difficult and dangerous journey. The camel caravans had to travel across great sandy deserts and over high mountains. Robbers often attacked the caravans. They killed the traders, and stole the camels and the precious cargoes.

The traders were afraid. "The journey to the East is too dangerous," they told the people.

But the people wanted the things from the East. "You must find a way—a way that is not so dangerous," they told the traders.

The traders thought about the problem. "If we could find a *waterway* to the East, the journey would not be so dangerous," they decided. "Is there some way to reach China and India by water? Is there a sea or an ocean that we have not heard about?"

The traders and the people began to think and to talk about a waterway to the East. "Perhaps if we sailed around Africa we could reach India," they said.

Prince Henry, the youngest son of the King of Portugal, believed the traders *could* reach India by sailing around Africa. He called to the palace the wisest men of Portugal. He also invited sailors who had traveled down the coast of Africa. For many days they studied maps and charts. They tried to learn all they could about the seas, the oceans, and the world. Perhaps Prince Henry *was* right!

Prince Henry sent many ships down the coast of Africa. But none of the sea captains dared travel far. They believed that if they traveled far enough the air would turn to fire, the sea to boiling water. No one was brave enough to travel around Africa and reach India. Prince Henry died without finding a waterway to the East!

People Seek Better Ways of Living. Years passed. A waterway to the East had not been found. But the people were not ready to give up! *They could not forget the story of Marco Polo's adventures.* They could not forget the stories told by the other travelers. They could not forget the beautiful things from the distant lands.

The more they thought about these things the more they wanted them. "The people in other parts of the world have better ways of living," they said. "We must have them, too." *The story of how these better ways of living were found is both strange and interesting.*

11

THINGS TO DO

1. Find a globe or a large map of the world. Locate Iceland, Greenland, India, China, Africa, Asia, and Europe. Show the class how men could reach India by sailing around Africa.

2. Find Venice and China on your globe or map. See if you can discover some of the reasons the Polos found it difficult to travel from Venice to China.

3. Make soap, wood, or clay models of Viking ships.

4. Dramatize the story of the Polos' returning to Venice.

5. Make a booklet and print "The Old World Finds the New" on the cover. Keep your booklet until you have finished reading all the stories about the discovery of America.

6. Pretend that you were present when Leif Ericson discovered Vinland. In your booklet draw a picture that shows some of the things you think he and his men did.

7. In your booklet draw a picture which will show something that happened during Marco Polo's stay in China or upon his return to Venice.

LET'S TALK ABOUT—

1. How Marco Polo's book made the people of Europe want to discover new ways to the East.

2. How the book helped them develop new ideas and new thoughts.

3. How the people of Europe began to change their ways of thinking and living after they read Marco Polo's book.

4. How Prince Henry and the sailors from Portugal tried to find a waterway to India.

5. How a book might have led to the discovery of America.

A WORD GAME

Here are some words that are used in the next story. They may be new to you. For each word there is a phrase that tells its meaning. Can you match the words and the phrases?

wharf — a large body of land

admiral — an officer who commands a group of ships

supplies — to understand

realize — a pier where ships are unloaded

continent — stores of food, clothing, and water

NAMES YOU WILL MEET IN THE NEXT STORY

Christopher Columbus	*Santa María*	Portugal
King Ferdinand	*Pinta*	San Salvador
Queen Isabella	*Niña*	Amerigo Vespucci

Before America was discovered, there were a few wise men who believed that the world is round. They believed that men could sail west, go around the world, and reach the East. But other people laughed at them. Nearly everyone believed that the earth was flat.

Even the people who believed that the earth is round had strange ideas. They believed that on the other side of the earth everything would be upside down. They thought that if they went there they would have to walk "head down." They thought they might even fall off the earth!

Then came a *voyage* that taught the people many things. After you have read this story, talk about what the voyage proved to the people. Talk about how the voyage helped to change their ideas about the world. Talk about how the voyage helped to make America as it is today.

THE OLD WORLD
FINDS THE NEW

COLUMBUS BELIEVES THE WORLD IS ROUND

Christopher Columbus was born in Genoa, Italy, many years ago. From the time he was a small boy, he loved the sea. Day after day he sat on the wharves and watched the ships sail into port. Day after day he watched the sailors unload the vessels. Day after day he waited for the time when he, too, could go to sea.

When he was fourteen years old, Columbus went to sea for the first time. After that he followed the sea for many years. Then he became a map maker in Portugal. While he was making maps, he studied the earth and the seas.

People were still looking for a waterway to the East. Columbus knew that most of the people believed that the earth was flat. He was not sure. As he studied about the earth and seas, he wondered. "Other sailors have tried to reach India by sailing east," he said to himself. "They have failed. If the earth is round, perhaps I can reach the East by sailing *west*, and *going around the world*."

The more Columbus thought about the idea, the more he believed in it. But he was a very poor man. He could not try his plan unless someone would help him. He went first to the King of Portugal. Then he asked some of the wealthy merchants of Genoa to help him. But no one would listen. "We cannot throw our money away on such a foolish idea," everyone said. "You will only fail."

Still Columbus would not give up. He asked for help in other Italian cities. No offers came. At last he went to Spain. He asked King Ferdinand and Queen Isabella to help him. But Spain was busy fighting a war.

"We need our money to buy food and supplies for our soldiers," said the Queen. "But I like your plan. Perhaps we can help you later."

Columbus waited for six long years before the King and Queen were ready to help him. Columbus asked for ships, men, and money. He asked for a share of the riches he might find and for the title of admiral. The King and Queen agreed.

Columbus was no longer a young man. His hair had turned white. His tall figure had grown bent, but his gray eyes flashed with happiness when the King and Queen agreed to help him. At last his dream was coming true!

COLUMBUS SETS SAIL

Columbus was given three ships, the *Santa María,* the *Pinta,* and the *Niña.* He finally found eighty-eight men who were willing to make the journey.

On August 3, 1492, the little ships sailed out of the harbor of Palos, Spain. The people of the town crowded the shore to wave good-by to the little company. Many of the people were crying. Some of the men on board ship were sad, too. Would they ever return home? *Would they ever again see their friends and families?*

For a time all went well. Columbus sailed to the west full of hope. Before long he expected to reach the shores of the Indies. But the long, weary hours became days. The days lengthened into weeks. Still the gray-blue water stretched on every side!

The men became frightened. "Why should we go on?" they said to one another. "Columbus is a madman. We cannot reach India by sailing *west.*"

They talked of seizing the ship and sailing back, but Columbus faced the angry men bravely. He talked to them and told them that they must go on—that they must find the Indies. The men grumbled. They muttered angrily, but finally they returned to their places on the ship.

More days passed. Still there was no sight of land! Again the men cried out in anger against Columbus. Again they begged him to return to Spain. Columbus gave only one answer, "We must sail on!"

One afternoon the sailors saw birds flying about the ship. They saw a green branch floating on the water. Some of the men began to sing. Others began to laugh and talk. Surely land could not be far away!

Night came. No one slept. Each man watched for some sign of land. About ten o'clock Columbus thought he saw a faint light in the distance. A little later a sailor said he had seen a light, too. The men waited eagerly.

The first gray dawn of morning came. It was *October 12, 1492.* The men crowded around the rails of the ships and peered into the distance. At first they could see nothing. Then a great cry arose, "Land! Land!" Before them lay a green island with people moving about on it.

Columbus ordered the boats lowered. He threw a red cloak around his shoulders, took the flag of Spain in his hand, and entered one of the boats.

When the men reached the shore, they fell to their knees and offered thanks to God. Then Columbus arose, drew his sword, and planted the flag of Spain on the shores of the new land. "I claim this land in the name of the King and Queen of Spain," he said. "I name it *San Salvador.*"

Columbus had discovered an island lying off the coast of America, but he thought he had found India or another part of the Indies. He named the people Indians. They are still called by that name.

For three months Columbus and his men sailed about. They discovered Cuba and several other islands. Then they returned to Spain.

Later Columbus made three other voyages to the lands he had discovered. Once he visited South America. Another time he sailed near the coast of Central America.

Columbus discovered the western half of the world, but he did not know it. He died without knowing he had made a wonderful discovery. He died without knowing he would always be remembered as the man who discovered America.

AMERICA IS NAMED

Not long after Columbus died, people realized that he had found a new land. Other men sailed to the new continent. One man, Amerigo Vespucci, said that he had made four trips to the New World. A map maker named the new land *America* in honor of Vespucci. "America" is our way of writing "Amerigo," Vespucci's first name.

Some people believe that Vespucci did not make the trips he wrote about. But the name "America" was kept for the new land. A little later men discovered that there were two large bodies of land in the western world. They named them North America and South America.

Columbus Leads the Way. The voyages made by Columbus proved that the other side of the world was not "upside down." They proved that there was no "jumping-off-place" —that ships would not sail to the "edge of the world" and fall off. They taught the people that there was another great continent across the ocean.

After Columbus discovered America, men were no longer so afraid to sail out upon the ocean. They traveled farther and farther from home. They explored new and distant lands. They discovered new ways of working and new and better ways of living.

Columbus led the way. Other men soon followed. The Old World found the New, and, little by little, ways of living began to change.

When he was a boy, Columbus watched the big ships sail into port. He dreamed of the day he, too, could become a sailor.

When grown, he made and studied maps. He believed the world is round. He thought he could sail west and go around the world.

But he needed help to prove his idea. No one would help until the King and Queen of Spain offered him both ships and money.

Columbus set sail in three ships, the *Santa María*, the *Pinta*, and the *Niña*. He sailed to the west hoping to find the Far East.

For days the ships sailed toward the west. Still there was no sign of land. The men wanted to turn back. Columbus refused.

At last, on the morning of October 12, 1492, Columbus and his men saw in the distance a green island looming on the horizon.

Columbus and his men found the island of San Salvador. They fell to their knees and thanked God for their safe arrival.

Holding the flag of Spain in his hand, Columbus took possession of the land for the King and the Queen of Spain.

Columbus and his men were sure they had reached an island off the coast of India. They called the people on the island Indians.

Columbus discovered the western half of the world. Later he made three other voyages to the new lands he had discovered.

NORTH AMERICA

EUROPE

AFRICA

Voyages Columbus made to the New World

SOUTH AMERICA

The third time he went to the New World, Columbus was unjustly blamed for things he did not do. He was sent home in chains.

Columbus did not know he had found a New World. A map maker named the new land America in honor of Amerigo Vespucci.

THINGS TO DO

1. Pretend that you are one of a group of sailors who lived at the time Columbus lived. Talk about why you would be afraid to sail out upon the ocean.

2. Ask your teacher to read the poem about Columbus that was written by Joaquin Miller. You will enjoy hearing it.

3. Act out some of the scenes from the story of Columbus. Decide which scenes you think will make the best play. Talk about what the actors should say and do. Try out your ideas. Do not write your play—just act it as you think it should be acted.

4. Make a chart that will tell the story of Columbus. Write sentences to explain your chart.

5. Add the story of Columbus to your booklet.

LET'S TALK ABOUT—

1. Columbus noticed that as a ship sails away it seems to sink into the water. This made him think that the earth is round. Can you tell why?

2. The men on Columbus' ship talked of seizing the ship and returning to Spain. Why did they not want to keep on sailing west?

3. Columbus discovered the New World, but he thought he had discovered a part of the Indies. Why do you think he thought he had discovered the Indies?

4. Columbus discovered the New World. Why was it not named for him? Why was it not called Columbia?

5. After the voyage of Columbus, people began to change their ways of living. How do you think the voyage helped?

6. The voyage of Columbus helped to make our country as it is today. How could this be true?

A WORD GAME

The words below are used in the next story. Each of the words has a phrase that explains it. Can you find the phrase that belongs to each word? You may use your dictionary.

settlement   a narrow strip of land that connects two larger bodies of land

rejoice   to name

strait   a little town or colony that has just been started

christen   a narrow passageway of water

pension   a sum of money given at regular times

isthmus   to be glad

NAMES YOU WILL MEET IN THE NEXT STORY

Isthmus of Panama   Ferdinand Magellan   Portuguese

Vasco Núñez de Balboa   Philippine Islands

The voyages of Columbus proved many things, but they did not prove one thing that men had wondered about. They did not prove that the world is round.

Columbus discovered the western half of the world, but another explorer proved that the world is round. After you have read this story, tell the class how the voyage of Magellan proved that the world is round. Talk about why the voyage was important. Talk about how it helped the people of that time to change their ways of living. Talk about how it helped our country to become as it is today.

A VOYAGE PROVES
THE WORLD IS ROUND

After Columbus made his voyages to America, other Spanish explorers sailed along the coast of South America. They helped to start little colonies there. The explorers were still seeking the rich cities of the Far East. They built the settlements as places where their ships could stop for repairs and supplies.

At that time the people thought the world was smaller than it is. When the explorers reached the shores of South America they thought the Far East could not be far away. "Surely," they said, "we have traveled far enough west to reach Asia in a few days or a few weeks." But ship after ship failed to find the Far East.

After a time the Spaniards began to realize that there were riches to be found in the New World. They did not find the sugar and the spices they had hoped to find in the Far East. But they found gold, silver, and other riches. They also found a mild climate, plenty of rain, and rich, fertile soil. The Spaniards began to grow sugar cane, spices, and tropical fruits. They started other settlements. Perhaps, in time, America would become as valuable as the Far East!

A NEW OCEAN IS FOUND

Vasco Núñez de Balboa was an early Spanish explorer. During his travels he came to what is now called Central

27

America. He found the little Spanish settlements that had been built there.

In the villages Balboa heard stories of a great sea to the south. "It is a sea that has never been seen by white men," the people told him. "We heard about it from the Indians. We also heard stories of gold and riches. But the sea, the gold, and the riches are across the isthmus. It is a difficult and dangerous journey."

Balboa laughed. He was not afraid. He took a party of men and started to cross the isthmus. But the journey was more difficult than he had thought! The land was covered with a dense jungle. For mile after mile the men had to cut their way through the matted underbrush! They had to watch for wild animals, snakes, and poisonous insects! They had to cross streams filled with alligators!

For days they fought the dangers of the jungle. Finally they came to the mountains that run through Panama. Balboa climbed to the top of the highest mountain peak. Eagerly he gazed toward the south and the west. It was true! There *was* a great sea to the south! Far in the distance stretched miles and miles of blue water. The water danced and sparkled in the bright sunshine.

For many minutes Balboa stood alone on the mountaintop. The blue sky outlined his tall, straight body. The gentle breeze rippled his brightly colored cloak. Balboa bowed his head in prayer. Then he turned and called to his men who were waiting on the mountainside.

"I have found it! I have found the great sea!" he shouted happily.

With loud cries the men rushed up the mountainside. They, too, saw the vast body of water. They shouted and rejoiced! Then a priest with the little party raised his voice. Suddenly the men became quiet. They dropped to their knees in prayer while the priest sang a song of praise. After the prayer was finished, Balboa spoke. He claimed the sea and all the land around it for the King and Queen of Spain.

The men wrote the claim on a piece of paper. Each man signed his name. Then they piled up a little heap of stones, on which they placed a wooden cross. In this way they hoped to prove that Spain could claim the great sea they had discovered.

After this the little party went on. The men went down the mountainside and through the green forests. At last they came to the sandy shores of the great ocean. Balboa wanted to touch the waters of the sea he had discovered. On a September day in 1513, he took the flag of Spain in his hand and walked out into the warm water. Once more he claimed the great ocean.

"I name this ocean the Great South Sea," he said in a voice that could be heard above the splashing of the waves. "I claim this ocean and all the land that touches it for the King and Queen of Spain."

Balboa discovered the South Sea, but the name he gave it was soon changed. Another explorer renamed it the *Pacific Ocean*.

Balboa heard the Indians of Central America tell of a great sea to the south. He wanted to claim the vast ocean for Spain.

He and his men started across the isthmus. They cut their way through dense jungles full of snakes, wild animals, and poisonous insects.

When they came to a tall range of mountains, Balboa climbed a high peak. Far away he saw the blue waters of a vast ocean.

Balboa called to his men waiting on the mountainside. "I have found the Great Sea!" he cried. The men hurried to join him.

Balboa and his men built a wooden cross, held high the flag of Spain, and claimed the ocean as part of the Spanish empire.

Later, Balboa walked into the warm waters of the South Sea and once again claimed the great ocean for the King of Spain.

Columbus believed the world is round. A Portuguese sea captain named Ferdinand Magellan proved that he was right. Magellan, like Columbus, believed that he could reach the Indies by sailing west. The King of Portugal would not help him, but the King of Spain gave him ships and money. This gave Spain the right to claim any lands Magellan might discover.

Balboa had discovered an ocean west of America. Magellan planned to sail along the coast of America and find a waterway to this ocean. Then he planned to sail *west across the ocean* and find the Indies.

It was a warm September morning in 1519. Five ships, their sails outspread, pulled away from the harbor in Spain. As the ships set out to sea, Magellan and his men waved proudly to the people on shore. The men were very happy. Soon they would find the waterway to the Far East. Soon they would return to Spain as heroes!

But the task was not so easy. Magellan searched and searched for a waterway to the South Sea. It was more than a year before he found one. He finally discovered a narrow waterway near the southern tip of South America. This waterway is called the *Strait of Magellan.*

By this time Magellan had lost one ship. The four

ships that were left sailed into the narrow passageway. In the strait another ship was lost. Only three sailed out into the great ocean.

When the men saw the ocean they gave loud shouts of joy. Magellan looked at the calm, peaceful waters and said to his men, "I christen this sea the *Pacific Ocean.*" "Pacific" means calm and peaceful. The ocean has been known by that name ever since.

But the sea was too calm! For weeks the ships made little progress. Food and drinking water became scarce. The men ate rats they caught on board ship. They soaked leather and ate it. They even ate sawdust!

Some of the men died. Others were so ill they could scarcely sail the ships. But at last they reached the Philippine Islands.

Magellan was killed in the Philippines, but the men decided to sail on. They burned one of the ships and sailed on in the other two. Finally they reached an island in the East Indies. Here another ship was found to be badly damaged. Only one ship was left to return to Spain.

The men loaded the ship with spices. They sailed across the Indian Ocean, around Africa, and home to Spain. The King gave each man a pension for life. He also gave the captain of the ship a globe of the world on which was printed "You Were the First to Sail around Me."

Magellan did not live to prove that the world is round, but the voyage he began is one of the greatest voyages of all time. His men sailed west from Spain. They kept sailing west until they sailed clear around the world and home again.

By always sailing west, they finally came back to the place from which they started. This proved beyond doubt that the world is round!

Magellan set sail with five ships to find the South Sea, sail across the ocean, and find the Indies. He, too, believed the world round.

He lost one ship near the coast of South America. He lost another as he passed through the strait that he discovered.

Three ships sailed into the calm waters of the vast South Sea. Magellan renamed the peaceful waters the Pacific Ocean.

34

Magellan and his men sailed across the Pacific Ocean to the Philippine Islands. Magellan was killed there, but his men went on, in two ships.

Magellan's men left one ship at an island in the Indies. They loaded the other ship with spices and sailed west to Spain.

By always sailing west, the men finally came back to the place from which they had started. This proved that the world is round.

THINGS TO DO

1. On a globe show the class how Magellan and his men sailed west from Spain, kept on sailing west, and finally reached Spain again.

2. Take a large sheet of wrapping paper. On the paper, have the class draw scenes that will tell the story of the voyage around the world.

3. Dramatize the story of Balboa. How do you think Balboa felt as he stood on the mountaintop and saw the great ocean for the first time? Make your actions and your words express this feeling.

4. Add the stories of Balboa and Magellan to the booklet you made after reading Story One.

5. Make a class time line. On your time line show the discoveries made by the early explorers. You have already read about some of them. As you think about the explorers, decide which events in their lives you think are the most important. Draw a picture that will represent each important event. Above the picture print the date the explorer visited America. Below the picture print the name of the explorer.

   Let the class choose the best picture to represent each explorer. Then paste the chosen pictures on a long sheet of paper and fasten it to the top of the blackboard. You will then have the first part of your time line of discovery. As you read about the other explorers, make new pictures to add to your time line.

LET'S TALK ABOUT—

1. Why Balboa's discovery of the Pacific was important to us.
2. How the voyage of Magellan proved that the world is round.

A WORD GAME

The phrases below tell the meaning of the words. Can you match the words and the phrases?

governor   the head of a state or territory

conquer   a group of nations united under one

wilderness   to take, usually by force

empire   country that has not been settled

NAMES YOU WILL MEET IN THE NEXT STORY

Juan Ponce de León   Peru

Hernando de Soto   Inca

Francisco Coronado

Spain was the first European country to claim land in the New World. In 1492 Columbus planted the flag of Spain on San Salvador. He found the New World while searching for a waterway to the Far East. Magellan also claimed land for Spain. He, too, was seeking a new route to the Far East when his men sailed around the world.

In this story you will read about Spanish explorers who visited America for other reasons. After you have read the story, talk about the reasons the other explorers came to America. Compare their journeys with the voyages of Magellan and Columbus. Talk about which explorers did the most to help our country become as it is today.

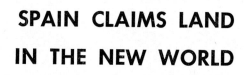

SPAIN CLAIMS LAND
IN THE NEW WORLD

A SOLDIER SEEKS YOUTH AND RICHES

Juan Ponce de León was a Spanish soldier who sailed with Columbus on one of his voyages to America. Later he returned to the island of Puerto Rico and became its governor. In Puerto Rico he heard the Indians tell of a distant land to the north.

"There are gold and riches there," the Indians said. "There is also a 'fountain of youth.' Anyone who bathes in the waters of this fountain will become young again."

Ponce de León did not realize that this could not be true. "If I can find this fountain, I will become young and strong again," he thought. He obtained permission from the King of Spain to search for the magic fountain.

In the spring of 1513, Ponce de León set sail from Puerto Rico. Soon after Easter Sunday he and his men reached the shores of North America. They found a beautiful land covered with flowers and green trees. Ponce de León claimed the land for the King and Queen of Spain. *He named it Florida.* In Spanish, *Pascua Florida* means Easter. *Florida* means "flowery" or "full of flowers."

Ponce de León and his men explored the countryside for many miles, but they did not find the magic fountain. They did not find gold or riches. Later Ponce de León was killed by an Indian, but *he was the first man to carry the flag of Spain into the mainland of North America.*

39

Ponce de León
heard tales of
riches in the
New World.
He also heard
the Indians
tell of a magic
"fountain of
youth."

Ponce de León
set sail for the
mainland of
North America.
He hoped to
find the magic
fountain and
become young
again.

Ponce de León
and his men
landed on the
coast of North
America. They
found a beauti-
ful land filled
with birds and
lovely flowers.

The men took
possession of
the land for
the King and
the Queen of
Spain. They
called this
beautiful new
land Florida.

For months the
men traveled
through the
wilderness of
Florida, but
they did not
find riches,
gold, nor the
magic fountain.

Ponce de León
was shot in
the back by
an Indian, but
he and his men
were the first
to claim land
in America for
Spain.

For many years the people of Europe talked of finding a waterway to the Far East. Then came another cry: "Gold! Gold! Gold! *The New World is a land filled with gold and riches!*" The waterway to the Far East was almost forgotten. Men sailed away to America in search of fame and fortune.

Some of the early Spanish explorers took soldiers and marched into Mexico, Central America, and South America. They conquered many of the Indian tribes who lived there.

Some of the Indian tribes were very wealthy. They had learned to farm the fertile lands and to mine the gold and silver in the hills. They had built splendid buildings, temples, and palaces. They had made beautiful ornaments of gold and silver. They had fashioned tools of copper and bronze, woven rich cloths, and made fine pottery.

The conquering Spaniards were not interested in the farms or the beautiful buildings. They wanted only wealth they could carry away. When they conquered the Indian tribes, they seized the Indian stores of gold and silver. They carried away everything that was of value.

Hernando de Soto was a bold Spanish explorer who helped to conquer the Inca Indians of Peru. His share of the gold that was taken from the Indians made him a very rich man. He returned to Spain and for a time lived like a king. But his money was soon gone.

De Soto did not want to be poor. He decided to sail to the New World again in search of another fortune. He had heard that Florida was a land of great beauty and great wealth. He obtained permission from the Spanish king to explore the country. Then he took a party of soldiers and sailed away.

42

De Soto and his men sailed first to Cuba. From there they sailed to the coast of North America. In 1539 they landed in Florida. For four long years they looked for gold and riches. They struggled through muddy swamps. They tramped through dense forests hung thick with moss. In their travels they covered much of the country that is now the southeastern part of the United States.

As they traveled through the wilderness, the Spaniards forced the Indian tribes to give them food. They made the Indian chieftains act as guides. It is little wonder that many of De Soto's men were killed by the Indians before their journey was over!

While he was still searching for gold, De Soto came to a great river. Its waters were swirling and rushing toward the sea. The Indians had named the river the Mississippi. In the Indian language, *misi* meant big and *sipi* meant river.

De Soto was the first white man to discover the lower part of the Mississippi River, but he was disappointed. He had not found the gold and riches he was seeking! He did not know that some day great cities would be built along the river's banks. He did not know that thousands of tons of goods would be carried upon its waters. *He did not know that the waters of the Mississippi were far more important to men than the discovery of gold!*

While on the banks of the river, De Soto became ill and died. His men did not want the Indians to know that their leader was gone. In the darkness of night they buried him. Quietly and gently they dropped his body into the muddy waters of the "big river."

De Soto's men did not stay in North America. They made their way down the Mississippi, across the ocean, and back home. *Their travels in the New World gave Spain the right to claim the territory they had explored.*

Hernando de Soto was a bold Spanish explorer. In 1539, he and his soldiers went to Florida to look for gold and riches.

For four years they tramped through forests and swamps. They traveled over most of what is now the southeastern United States.

In his search for gold, De Soto had constant trouble with the Indians. Many of his soldiers were killed by them.

While he was still looking for gold, De Soto reached the Mississippi. He was the first white man to see the lower half of it.

Although he had explored and claimed much territory for Spain, he was not happy. He had not found the gold he wanted.

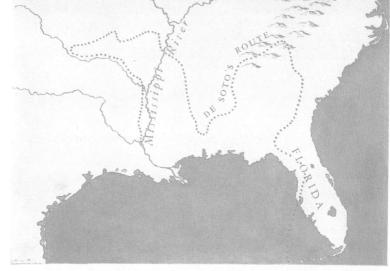

While on the banks of the Mississippi, De Soto died. His men buried him at night in the waters of the river he had discovered.

A SPANIARD EXPLORES THE SOUTHWEST

After the New World was discovered, many Spaniards went to live in Mexico. They liked the new land very much. It reminded them of the country they had left in Europe.

About the time De Soto was landing in Florida, the Spaniards in Mexico heard stories of rich lands to the north. One story said that there was a fabled land called Cibola. In Cibola there were seven cities. In these cities the houses were covered with gold and precious jewels.

The governor of Mexico sent a Spanish captain, Francisco Coronado, to find the fabled cities. With Coronado went horsemen in armor, well-armed foot soldiers, and Indian and Negro servants. The men took with them flocks of sheep, herds of cattle, and dozens of mules to carry the packs.

As Coronado and his men rode away, bands played and flags waved. But the gayety of the day was soon forgotten.

Before long the men came to the unsettled lands of the north. Day after day they tramped through the wilderness. Day after day they searched for the jeweled cities. They found seven cities, but the cities were only Indian pueblos with houses built of mud.

On their travels Coronado and his men saw the Grand Canyon of the Colorado. They marched through land that is now Arizona, New Mexico, Texas, Oklahoma, and Kansas, but they did not find gold or riches.

The men became tired and hungry. "We want to go home," they said to Coronado. "Our horses are worn out. Our clothes are old and ragged. Our food supply is low. We have been in many battles with the Indians. We can go no farther. There are no jeweled cities."

Coronado was very sad, but he gave the order to return home. He felt that his journey had failed. *Yet it was this journey that gave Spain the right to claim the southwestern part of North America!*

The Old World Learns More about the New. There were other Spaniards who explored both North and South America. Most of them were searching for gold. Some of them found what they were seeking. Others failed. But they all helped to explore new territory. They all helped to establish a large Spanish empire in the New World.

As they traveled throughout the country, the explorers learned many things about America. They learned that the soil was rich and fertile. They learned that there were great forests, stores of minerals, and many waterways here.

Because of all these things, people came here to live. They cleared the forests, planted crops, and built homes. They started little towns and cities. *They established the beginnings of the country that is now the United States.*

Francisco de Coronado was a Spanish captain who lived in Mexico. He heard stories of jeweled cities in fabled Cibola.

Coronado, his soldiers, and his servants rode away toward the north. They wanted to find the seven golden cities of Cibola.

Coronado and his men found seven cities, but they were only Indian pueblos, with houses built of adobe. The men rode on.

During their travels they came to the Grand Canyon, but they found no gold nor riches. The men were tired and heartsick.

Wearily they marched across what is now Arizona, New Mexico, Texas, Oklahoma, and Kansas. Finally they returned home.

Coronado felt he had failed. But it was his journey that gave Spain her claim to the southwestern part of the United States.

THINGS TO DO

1. As a class project, make a large map of North and South America. Trace in the territory claimed by the Spaniards. Color it orange. Save the map. After you have read the next story you will want to color the claims of France, England, and Holland.

2. Act out the story of Ponce de León. Think of the things he might say and do. Let a number of pupils take turns at acting the part of Ponce de León. Choose the pupil you think made the part seem most real.

3. Make a series of pictures entitled "The Spaniards Explore the New World." Under each picture write a sentence that will explain how the Spanish explorers helped our country become as it is today.

4. Add the stories of Ponce de León, De Soto, and Coronado to your booklet.

5. Add the Spanish explorations to your class time line.

LET'S TALK ABOUT—

1. Why the discovery of the Mississippi River was more important than the discovery of gold.

2. Why the Spanish explorations are a part of the story of the United States.

3. How the Spanish explorers helped us, and helped our country to become as it is today.

A NEW WORD GAME

You will find many new words in this book. Some of the words will be the names of *persons* or *places*. Others may be words that describe *events* or *history terms*. Find a large box and make a class file for the new words you learn as you study the story of America. Decorate the box with pictures that represent some of the explorers.

Divide your word file into sections. One section might be labeled "persons." Another might be labeled "places," and so on. After your file is ready, put into it the new words you learn. When you put a word card into your file, you may wish to decorate it to make it more interesting.

NAMES YOU WILL MEET IN THE NEXT STORY

You will meet the following names in the next story. After you have read about these persons or places you may wish to make word cards for your file.

Jacques Cartier	Louis Jolliet	Robert La Salle
Jesuit	Quebec	Newfoundland
Labrador	John Cabot	Father Marquette
	Samuel de Champlain	

Before You Read the Story—

Spain was not the only European country interested in the New World. Explorers from France, England, and Holland also visited America. Some of them came here even before the Spanish explorers you have read about. They explored different parts of the New World and claimed land for their countries.

Some of the explorers were searching for a waterway to the Indies. Others came here for different reasons. After you have read this story, talk about why each explorer came here and how he helped his country. Talk about how all the explorers helped us.

FRANCE, ENGLAND, AND HOLLAND CLAIM LAND

CARTIER DISCOVERS THE ST. LAWRENCE

In 1534 France sent Jacques Cartier to look for a waterway through North America. Cartier touched Newfoundland—then sailed along the coast of North America until he came to a great gulf and river. It was the Gulf of St. Lawrence and the St. Lawrence River.

Cartier anchored his ships near the mouth of the river. Then he and his men climbed the rolling hill beside the harbor. They set up a large wooden cross on which was nailed a board bearing the words "Long Live the King of France." In this way they claimed the river and all the land around it for France.

Then the men returned to France to make their report. "We saw open waters leading to the west," Cartier said. "Perhaps it is a waterway through North America."

The King was encouraged and gave Cartier money for a second voyage. The next year Cartier went again to the St. Lawrence. He followed the river west for many miles, but he did not find a waterway. When winter came, his men built a fort where Quebec, Canada, stands today. The winter was bitter cold. There was little food. The men were glad to return to France in the spring.

Cartier made other trips to America, but *he helped his country most by planting the cross of France beside the St. Lawrence.*

Jacques Cartier lived in a little fishing town in France. He listened to the fishermen tell stories of a wonderful land across the sea.

In 1534, the King of France sent Cartier to explore the New World and look for a waterway through North America.

Cartier discovered the St. Lawrence River and the Gulf of St. Lawrence. He claimed the waters and all the land nearby for France.

He left the New World to return to France. "The river may be a waterway to the Indies," he told the King.

The King gave Cartier money for other voyages to America. Cartier and his men sailed up the St. Lawrence for many miles.

They did not find a waterway through North America, but they were the first men to claim land in America for France.

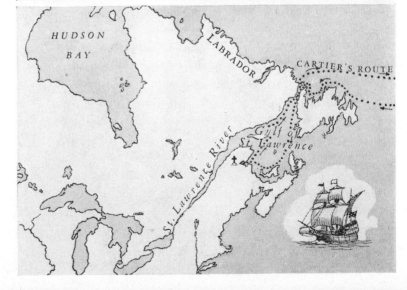

FRENCH SETTLERS COME TO AMERICA

Even before Cartier discovered the St. Lawrence, French fishermen had come to America. They crossed the Atlantic to fish in the waters near Newfoundland and Labrador. Each time they returned to France they told wonderful stories about the New World.

In a little town on the coast of France lived a boy named Samuel de Champlain. The boy liked to watch the fishing boats as they returned from the New World. He liked to hear the stories of the fishermen. What a wonderful place the New World must be! What fun it would be to sail away to the new land filled with gold and riches!

When he was grown, Champlain became a sailor and a map maker. He learned how to explore a coastline or a country and how to put what he had learned on a map. Like other men he, too, wanted to find a waterway through North America. He wanted to make a map of the waterway so other sailors could also find it.

In 1603 he went to the St. Lawrence Valley for the first time. He went back again the next year and continued to make maps of the country.

The winters were long and cold in the New World. Many of Champlain's men became sick. About half of them died. Champlain talked with the men who were left.

W. C. MERRITT

"It is not enough just to explore the country," he said. "We must learn to *live* in the New World. We must raise vegetables and grain and store them away for the winter. We must build better houses. We must plan for the long, cold months ahead."

The men worked hard and planned wisely. By their third winter in the New World they were well and happy. They explored the St. Lawrence Valley and part of the Atlantic seacoast. Champlain made maps of the country for other explorers to use.

Then he decided it was time for his men to build a real town. "I know just the right place for a settlement," he said to himself. "Up the river is a giant rock on the bank of a stream. Years ago Cartier and his men spent a winter under the rock. They were well sheltered from the cold. It is a good place for a town."

When the men saw the place Champlain had chosen, they were pleased. "You have chosen well," they said to their leader. In the spring they set to work to build a town and prepare for the long winter ahead.

Some of the men planted grain and vegetables. Others built a high fort. On each side of it they built houses. The houses were built close to the fort so the settlers could reach the fort quickly if the Indians attacked.

Champlain called his settlement *Quebec*. He became governor of the little colony and ruled wisely and well. He also explored the country and drew maps of the new land. On one of his trips he discovered the blue waters of Lake Champlain. He also sailed into the waters of Lake Ontario and Lake Huron. He did not find a waterway through North America, but he taught settlers how to live in the new land. *He established a strong French colony in the New World.*

As a boy, Samuel de Champlain was interested in stories of the New World. When grown, he became a map maker and an explorer.

In 1603, he went to the St. Lawrence Valley. He wanted to find a waterway through America and make a map of it for others.

The winters were long and cold there. The men could not keep warm. Many of them became sick and many of them died.

In the summer
Champlain told
his men, "We
must learn to
build homes,
plant crops,
and plan for
the long, cold
winter ahead."

Champlain and
his men built
a settlement
where the town
of Quebec now
stands. The
men chose
Champlain as
their governor.

Champlain was
a good gover-
nor. He did not
find a water-
way to the East
Indies, but he
began the first
French settle-
ment in Amer-
ica.

MARQUETTE AND JOLLIET EXPLORE THE MISSISSIPPI

Soon after the French explorers claimed land in the New World, French missionaries sailed to America. The missionaries were Jesuit priests. The priests traveled far into the forests and taught the Indians about the Christian religion. They also explored much of the country. Later they wrote stories about their journeys and made maps of the places they visited.

Father Marquette was a Jesuit priest who lived in an Indian village on the shores of Lake Michigan. In 1673 a young fur trader named Louis Jolliet came to see him.

"The governor of Quebec wants me to explore the Mississippi River," he told Father Marquette. "He thinks the Mississippi may be a waterway to the Pacific Ocean. Will you go with me?"

Father Marquette was eager to go with Jolliet. They took five other men and set out in two birch-bark canoes. Across the lake, across Green Bay, and into the Fox River they paddled their canoes. They followed the Fox River as far as they could go. Then they carried their canoes to the Wisconsin River. The Wisconsin River brought them into the swirling waters of the Mississippi.

Father Marquette's heart was filled with joy as the canoes sailed onto the waters of the broad river. The other men were glad, too. "We shall see where the river leads," they said to one another.

For many days the men paddled their canoes down the swift waters of the great river. Finally they came to the place where the Arkansas River flows into the Mississippi. By this time they realized that the river did not flow to the west. It was not a waterway to the Pacific!

The men turned back. Father Marquette went back

60

to his home. Jolliet went on to report to the governor of Quebec. The two Frenchmen did not find a waterway to the Pacific, but *they did claim much of the Mississippi Valley for France.*

LA SALLE REACHES THE MOUTH OF THE MISSISSIPPI

Robert La Salle was another brave French explorer. When he heard of the journey made by Marquette and Jolliet, he decided to follow the Mississippi to its mouth. He took with him both white men and Indians.

In February, 1682, they set sail upon the muddy waters of the Mississippi. For days they floated and paddled down the river in their canoes. As they traveled farther south, the water began to look different. It tasted salty.

"The ocean waters are meeting the waters of the river," the men said. "We are nearing the mouth of the Mississippi."

In April they reached the mouth of the great river. It was a happy day for La Salle and his men. At last they had reached the gulf. France could claim the honor of following the Mississippi to its mouth.

The men marched to the highest point near the river. They planted a wooden cross in the soil and laid beside it the arms of France. Then La Salle raised his sword. "I take possession of this river, all the waters that enter it, and all the lands watered by it," he said. "I take possession in the name of Louis XIV, the King of France. I name this country Louisiana."

La Salle planted the cross of France at the mouth of the Mississippi. Cartier planted it on the Gulf of the St. Lawrence. The two crosses planted by the explorers were far apart, but *they marked the beginning of a large French empire in the New World.*

61

Marquette and Jolliet started out to explore the Mississippi. They wanted to see if the river was a water-way to the Pacific.

They paddled across Green Bay, and to the end of the Fox River. Then they carried their canoes to the Wisconsin River.

The Wisconsin brought them to the Mississippi. They paddled on but turned back when they found the river did not lead to the West.

When Robert La Salle heard of the journey of Jolliet and Marquette, he decided to go to the mouth of the great river.

He took with him both Indians and white men. They went on and on until they came to the place the river met the sea.

La Salle stood near the mouth of the river. He claimed the river and the land around it for France. He called the land Louisiana.

63

CABOT CLAIMS LAND FOR ENGLAND

John Cabot sailed to America in search of gold and a waterway to China. He explored along the shores of Greenland and Labrador and along part of the Atlantic coast.

He did not find a waterway, nor did he find gold. But when he returned to England he brought stories of a new wealth. "The fish are so plentiful along the coast of North America that they can be lifted out of the sea in baskets," he told the people.

For many years the fishermen of Europe sailed to the New World. They built up a rich fishing industry. Cabot's journey gave England new wealth, but it also gave her something even more important. It gave England the right to claim most of the Atlantic seacoast.

The voyages made by Cabot brought wealth to England and gave her the right to claim much of the Atlantic Coast of North America.

John Cabot sailed to America to find gold and a waterway to China. He was the first man to claim land for the English.

Cabot explored along the Atlantic Coast of North America and along the shores of Labrador. He found great schools of fish.

For many years fishing boats from Europe sailed to the New World. The fishermen built up a rich fishing industry.

FRANCIS DRAKE SAILS AROUND THE WORLD

The Spanish explorers conquered many of the Indian tribes of South America. They seized the Indian stores of gold, silver, and other wealth. Then they loaded the stolen treasures on ships and sailed back to Spain.

Before long, sea captains from other countries began to trade with the Spanish colonies in the New World. They also attacked the Spanish ships returning to Spain and robbed them of their rich treasures. Spain was very angry, and there were many fierce sea battles between the Spanish ships and ships from other countries.

An English sea captain named Francis Drake made several voyages to the New World to trade with the Spanish colonies. At one time he traveled across the Isthmus of Panama. While on the isthmus, he climbed a tall tree and looked to the west. From the treetop, he saw for the first time the blue waters of the Pacific.

As he looked at the peaceful water, Drake's heart was filled with a great desire. "No English ship has ever sailed the Pacific," he said half aloud. "God grant that I may live to sail upon its waters."

In 1577 Drake sailed again from England to make his dream come true. In his fleet were five small ships and about one hundred sixty men. When he reached Brazil, he left two of the ships there. The other three sailed on to the Strait of Magellan. It took sixteen days for the ships to pass through the strait. Then a storm separated the vessels, and Drake was left alone with only his flagship. He was sorry to lose his other ships, but his dream had at last come true. An English ship was sailing the waters of the blue Pacific!

Drake's ship was first called the *Pelican*. Later he renamed it the *Golden Hind*. The *Golden Hind* sailed up the coast of South America. The Spaniards were not expecting to see an English ship in the Pacific. Drake surprised them and captured many riches. When the *Golden Hind* was bulging with treasure, Drake wanted to return to England. But he did not dare go back through the strait. He knew the Spanish ships would be waiting for him.

There was only one thing to do. He must follow the path of Magellan's men—cross the Pacific and sail around the world. During his journey Drake landed on the shores of California. He claimed the land for England and then sailed on. The *Golden Hind* crossed the broad Pacific. Then it sailed across the Indian Ocean, around the southern tip of Africa, and northward to England on the Atlantic Ocean. An Englishman had sailed around the world! *He had also claimed land on the western coast of North America.*

The angry Spaniards called Drake the "Master Thief of the Unknown World," but the Queen of England made him a knight. She gave him the title *Sir Francis Drake.*

Other English explorers also came to the New World. Most of them failed in what they tried to do. But they opened the way for men to come here later and build homes.

Spanish ships loaded with riches taken from the South American Indians were often attacked by ships from other countries.

Francis Drake, an Englishman, also wanted riches from South America. With five little ships, he set sail for the Pacific.

Drake left two of his ships in Brazil. He lost two more after going through the Strait of Magellan. Then he had only his flagship.

Drake renamed his ship the *Golden Hind*. Then he sailed up the coast of South America. He seized Spanish ships and treasures.

At one time he landed on the coast of California. He claimed the land for England. Then he wanted to return home.

He crossed the Pacific and Indian oceans. He went around Africa, through the Atlantic to England. He had gone around the world!

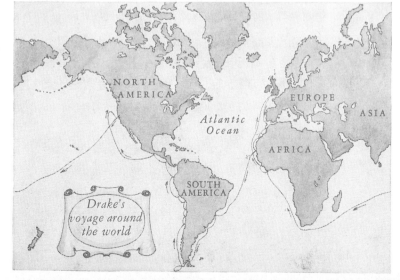

Drake's voyage around the world

HUDSON CLAIMS LAND FOR HOLLAND

It was an interesting ship that sailed through the stormy waters of the wide Atlantic. It was a ship bright with color. Part of it was painted red, part of it green, part of it yellow, and part of it blue like the sky. On the blue part, stars and a moon had been painted.

The name of the ship was the *Half Moon*. The flag that flew proudly from its mast was *Dutch*. The captain of the ship was Henry Hudson, an *English* sea captain. Hudson was an Englishman, but he was sailing to America for a Dutch trading company. This meant that any lands he might discover would belong to Holland.

The little ship sailed on and on until it sailed into the harbor that is now New York harbor. As the ship docked, Indians crowded the shore. In their hands they carried tobacco leaves. They wanted to trade with the white men. Hudson gave them beads and knives for their tobacco. Then he claimed the land for Holland.

Hudson was looking for a waterway through North

America. While searching for it, he found the river that flows into New York harbor. Today it is called the Hudson River. Hudson sailed up the river until it became so narrow he could go no farther. He realized it was not a waterway to the Pacific, so he returned to Europe.

Hudson did not find a waterway to the Pacific, but he helped Holland. *His voyage gave the Dutch their claim to land in America.*

Later Hudson sailed under the flag of England. On this journey he discovered Hudson Bay and Hudson Strait. But winter came while he was in the bay. Ice formed quickly and caught his ships fast. The men on board suffered greatly from the cold and from hunger. They became very angry with Hudson. When the ice melted enough so the ship could move, they put Hudson, his son, and seven of the sailors in a little open boat. The big ship sailed away to England. The little boat was left among the ice cakes!

The Story Goes on. The Old World had found the New! Explorers from France, Spain, England, and Holland had discovered new and rich lands across the sea. They had taught the people of Europe many things about America. The explorers had awakened interest in the new land, but *their* work in the story of America was finished.

Who was to come next? America had been discovered. Now it was time to build homes in the New World. It was time to build towns and cities. It was time to begin building our country into the nation it is today.

The rest of this book is the story of the men and women who helped to build our country. It is the story of the men and women *who made possible all the things we have today.* They are interesting people. You will enjoy reading about them.

The little ship, the *Half Moon*, sailed into New York Harbor. It was a Dutch ship sailed by an English sea captain, Henry Hudson.

As the ship anchored, Indians crowded the shore. They held tobacco leaves in their hands. They wanted to trade with the Dutch.

After trading with the Indians, Hudson claimed the land for Holland. Then he sailed on. He found the river we call the Hudson.

Later, Hudson sailed for England. He discovered Hudson Bay and Hudson Strait. But winter came and his ship caught fast in the ice.

Hudson's men were angry. When the ice melted, they put him, his son, and seven sailors in a little boat and sailed away.

Hudson was not heard from again, but his voyages gave both Holland and England the right to claim land in America.

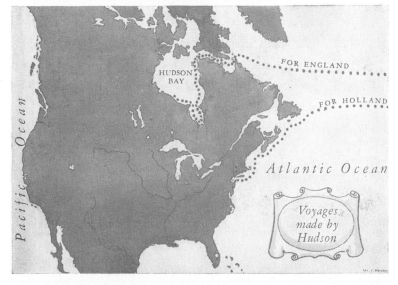

FOR ENGLAND

HUDSON BAY

FOR HOLLAND

Pacific Ocean

Atlantic Ocean

Voyages made by Hudson

THINGS TO DO

1. On the map you drew for the last story, color the claims of France, England, and Holland. Color the claims of France blue, the claims of England green, and the claims of Holland yellow.

2. Write a short story about your favorite explorer. In your story, tell why you like him best. Tell what he did when he came to the New World.

3. Make a group of pictures that will tell the story of each explorer you have read about. Use your pictures in a travelogue. A travelogue is an illustrated talk about people's travels. As you show your pictures to another class, have someone explain what each picture means.

4. Have you ever played charades? When you play charades you act out a word. The others are supposed to guess the word you are acting. Play a game called "Explorer Charades." Act out scenes from the life of one of the explorers. Let the class try to guess whose life you are acting out.

5. Add to your booklet the explorers you have read about in this story.

6. Add the stories of Cartier, Champlain, Jolliet, Father Marquette, La Salle, Cabot, Drake, and Hudson to your class time line.

7. You have finished reading Part One of *America's Own Story*. This part of the book is about the explorers who discovered America. After the story of each explorer is a picture story that tells about his travels. Beginning with the Vikings, have a "picture study" of all the explorers you have read about in Part One. Discuss their travels, the clothes they wore, the ships they sailed in, and other interesting things the pictures tell you. In your picture study include the review on pages 76 and 77, the time line on page 78, and the map on page 79.

LET'S TALK ABOUT—

1. Why each of the explorers you have read about in this story came to the New World.

2. How the explorers helped their country and how they helped us.

3. Why the work of all the explorers was important to us.

4. How the explorers helped our country to become as it is today.

5. Why the story of America does not end with the discovery and exploration of the New World.

A WORD GAME

Make a list of the new words you have learned while reading Part One. Are there any words you wish to add to your word file?

The words listed below are in the next story. If you do not understand them, look them up in your dictionary.

diorama	valuable	habitant
hacienda	plaza	explosion

NAMES YOU WILL MEET IN THE NEXT STORY

St. Augustine   *El Camino Real*   Santa Fe

Vikings discover America, but tell no one.

Balboa discovers the Pacific Ocean.

Polo's book makes men seek new ways to East.

Magellan's men sail around the world.

Columbus discovers the New World in 1492.

Ponce de León claims Florida for Spain.

The New World is named America.

De Soto reaches the Mississippi River.

Coronado explores the Southwest for Spain.

La Salle reaches the mouth of the Mississippi.

Cartier discovers the St. Lawrence.

John Cabot claims land for England.

Champlain builds first French settlement.

Sir Francis Drake sails around the world.

Marquette and Jolliet explore the Mississippi.

Hudson claims land for Holland and England.

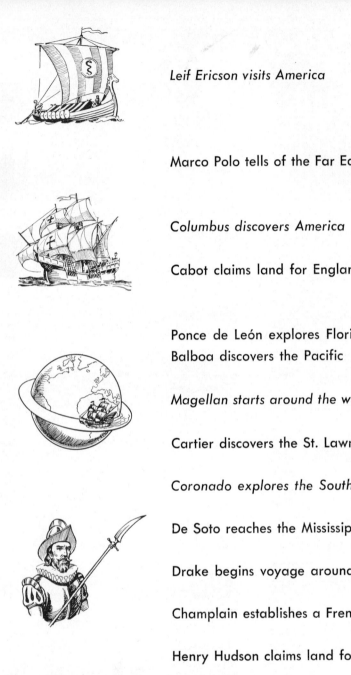

Leif Ericson visits America	1000
Marco Polo tells of the Far East	1295
Columbus discovers America	1492
Cabot claims land for England	1497
Ponce de León explores Florida	1513
Balboa discovers the Pacific	1513
Magellan starts around the world	1519
Cartier discovers the St. Lawrence	1536
Coronado explores the Southwest	1540
De Soto reaches the Mississippi	1541
Drake begins voyage around the world	1577
Champlain establishes a French colony	1608
Henry Hudson claims land for Holland	1609
Marquette and Jolliet explore Mississippi	1673
La Salle reaches mouth of Mississippi	1682

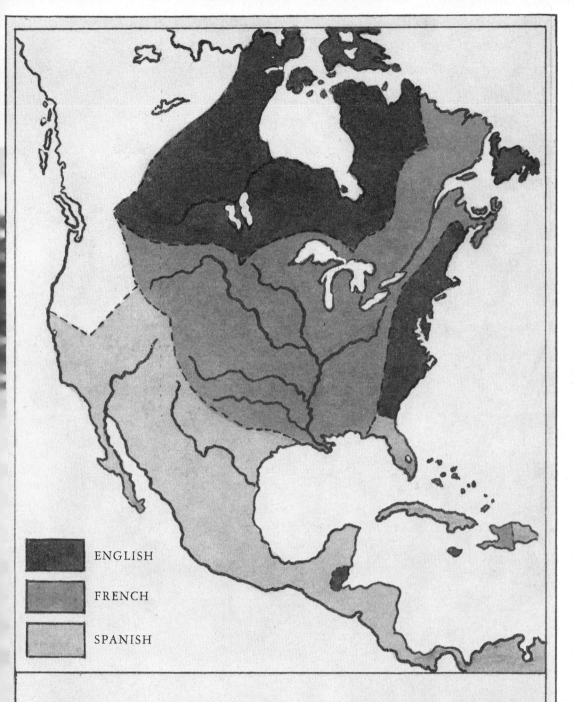

ENGLISH

FRENCH

SPANISH

English explorers claimed land on the Atlantic seacoast and around Hudson Bay. The French claimed the Mississippi Valley and the land around the St. Lawrence. Spanish explorers claimed Mexico, the Southwest, and Florida.

Part II—OUR COUNTRY BEGINS

Before You Read the Story—

Spain, France, England, and Holland had claimed land in the New World. Brave and daring explorers from each of these countries had traveled over much of the land that is now the United States. They had gone back to Europe and had told the people about the wonders of the new land.

Before long, people from the Old World began to build homes in America. They began to clear the forests, plant crops, and settle the wilderness. But their task was not easy. They had many difficult times.

After you have read this story, talk about why it was difficult for the settlers to build homes in the New World. Talk about why their task was as difficult as the task of the explorers. Compare the Spanish, the French, and the English colonies.

Story One

HOMES
IN THE NEW WORLD

Explorers from Spain, France, and England claimed land in the New World. Each country had large and valuable holdings. But it was not enough just to *claim* the land. The land had to be *settled*.

The first settlers were as brave and as daring as the explorers. They had to build homes where great forests stood. They had to build roads where there were only rough trails. They had to clear land and raise food. It was a task that took great courage and hard work!

THE SPANISH SETTLERS

In 1565 the King of Spain sent soldiers to protect Florida from the French. Many of the soldiers stayed. They built homes and began the town of St. Augustine, Florida. A little later, Spaniards from Mexico settled the town of Santa Fe, New Mexico. *St. Augustine and Santa Fe are the two oldest cities in the United States.*

The Spanish settlements were in the southern part of the United States. Some were in Florida. Others were as far away as California. Between their settlements, the Spaniards built many roads and trails. In California, the road was called *El Camino Real*, or the King's Highway.

Some of the Spanish settlements were very interesting. Perhaps the most interesting were the small farming villages, the haciendas, and the missions.

A farming village was a little town laid out around a square called the *plaza*. Near the plaza were a few good houses for the officials sent over from Spain, a palace for the governor, and a fort for some of the soldiers. The other houses in the village were usually built of mud, but the people who lived in them were not unhappy. In the evening they often gathered in the plaza and sang and danced or visited with their neighbors.

Outside the village were small farms owned by the *rancheros*, or farmers. Most of the rancheros were soldiers. A foot soldier usually had a small piece of ground for a garden, a small orchard, a pasture for cattle, and a little land on which he grew wheat, barley, and corn. If the ranchero happened to be a mounted soldier, his farm was larger.

An *hacienda* was a very large estate, or a grant of land, given to a man by the king. It was usually given to him because he had served in the army. In the center of the hacienda was a great house where the proud owner and his family lived a happy, carefree life. In the big house there was always dancing, music, or gayety. The happy people thought little about the Indians who did all the work.

The Indian servants lived in little huts near the big house. The men herded the thousands of cattle that roamed the big estate. They tended the gardens and orchards, and did all the heavy work about the estate. The Indian women worked in the big kitchen grinding grain, baking bread, and cooking food. They kept the big house clean and waited on the owner, his family, and his guests.

The *missions* were established by the Catholic priests who came to teach and to help the Indians. The main part of the mission was a large courtyard surrounded by strong walls. At one end of the courtyard was a beautiful church.

84

Near the church were adobe houses where the priests lived. Farther away were the workshops of the Indians.

In the workshops, the Indian men made saddles, bridles, and riding boots. They cut stone for the churches. They prepared beef for drying and filled the storehouses with food for winter.

The Indian women worked, too. They spun cloth and sewed beautiful garments for the priests. They dipped candles to burn at the altar and did all the work about the mission courtyard.

Outside the mission courtyard was a large piece of land where the Indians lived, tilled the fields, and tended herds of cattle. There was also a fort where soldiers stood constant guard.

There were many such missions in California and the Southwest. These missions were not only churches. They were settlements where people lived, worked, and worshiped.

FRENCH SETTLERS IN AMERICA

Many of the early French settlers who came to America were traders. In the wintertime they hunted and trapped in the forests. In the spring they traded with the Indians. It was always a colorful and interesting sight during trading week. Before the trading began, swift runners went deep into the forests. "The white men are ready to trade," was the word they passed from one tribe to another.

The Indians were pleased. This was the day they had been waiting for! They donned their brightest beads and feathers. They put on their gayest costumes. Then they loaded their birch canoes with their winter's catch of furs and pushed off down the river.

As the time for trading drew near, canoe after canoe paddled softly into the trading post. After the canoes were safely landed, the Indians and the white men smoked the pipe of peace. Then the red men traded their rich, soft furs for the guns, powder, knives, and other articles offered by the white men.

Most of the traders grew rich and went back to France. The people who really settled the land for the French were the farmers, or *habitants*, who lived in Canada and Louisiana. The farms of the habitants were laid out along the fertile riverbanks. Each farmer had a long, narrow strip of land. One end of the land faced the flowing river; the other ran back to the green forest.

Along the bank of the river was a narrow road. The houses of the habitants were built in a row along this road. This made it seem as if a town were built along the riverbank. It also made life easier for the people. Each family had close neighbors. The road between the houses was well worn by playing children and by grown-up people visiting and helping one another.

The houses of the habitants were built of wood or stone. They were whitewashed to make them look fresh and clean. The furniture inside the house was very simple and most of it was homemade. There were chairs, beds, a large table, and a cradle. The habitants liked large families. There was nearly always a baby cooing and laughing in the cradle by the fireplace.

On the wall of the little house hung a gun and a powder horn. The habitants had cleared the land and made farms. But they had to protect their homes against wild animals and unfriendly Indians.

The people worked hard but they had many happy times. On Sundays and on feast days they visited, danced, and played cards. On the wall in nearly every home hung a fiddle. In the evening the strains of sweet music could often be heard along the riverbanks.

The habitants did not come to the New World to get rich. They loved their homes and their families. They were satisfied to live simple but happy lives.

On an April day in 1607 three small ships sailed up a wide river on the east coast of North America. The ships carried more than one hundred Englishmen. Four months earlier the men had sailed from England to start a colony in the New World. During the long journey they had grown tired and restless. Now the sight of land and green trees filled them with joy.

The men sailed up the river looking for a place to build a settlement. Finally they dropped anchor near a wooded point of land. "Here is the place to build our settlement," they said. They called it Jamestown, Virginia. They named the river James in honor of King James.

Before the men left England, a council of leaders had been appointed to guide the colony. For a while the men worked well under their leaders. They built a fort, a church, and some houses. Then they grew lazy and quarrelsome. Instead of growing crops, they searched for gold.

As the summer passed, the men grew more and more quarrelsome. The place they had chosen for a settlement was low and marshy. Drinking water was scarce. Some of the men became ill with fever. Others sat idly by.

The leaders were worried, but they could do little. Winter came. There was not enough food to feed the hungry men. Captain John Smith, one of the leaders of the colony, went to the Indians to ask for food. The Indians were unfriendly and for a time it looked as if Smith might be put to death. Then the chieftain changed his mind and gave Smith food to take back to the starving men.

In a short while Smith was made president of the council. He proved to be a wise and a strong leader. "The men who do not work shall not eat," he commanded. "We shall feed the sick, but the well must work." Many of the men who had hunted for gold turned to farming. In the spring they plowed the ground and planted crops.

Then Smith was burned in a gunpowder explosion and went back to England for treatment. Under new leaders, the men soon fell back into their lazy ways.

When another winter came, the food was soon gone. In the little houses the men lay sick and dying. A few of them kept alive by eating roots and fish, but most of them starved to death. In the story of Virginia, that winter is called the *Starving Time*.

In the spring, more men and new leaders came over from England. But for a few years times were still difficult. Then conditions began to change. The settlers learned how to grow tobacco and how to cure it. They discovered they could sell it in England for a high price. Negro slaves were brought into the colony to work in the fields.

Women came over from England. The men married the women and made homes. With homes and families to care for, the men forgot their desire to search for gold. They worked hard to make the colony prosper.

In time, Jamestown, the little colony that nearly failed, grew and became rich.

A New Country Is Begun. The first settlers had come to America. They had started homes in the New World. A new chapter in the story of our country had begun. The early settlers suffered many hardships, but they had faith in the new land. They stayed. From the small beginning they made, grew a great country!

Other settlers followed the ones you have read about. These settlers, too, had difficult times. But they all helped to begin the country that is now the United States.

In 1607, the first English settlers went to Virginia. The men built a settlement and called it Jamestown in honor of King James.

At first the men worked well. Then they grew lazy. When the winter came, their food was soon gone. The men were cold, ill, and hungry.

John Smith, one of the leaders of the colony, went to the Indians and obtained food for the starving men of Jamestown.

In the spring Smith told the lazy men, "No work, no food!" Then Smith returned to England. Again the men would not work.

Later, under new leaders, life grew better. Women from England came to the colony to help the men make homes.

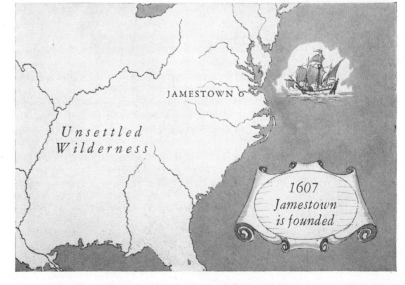

The men soon learned how to grow tobacco and other crops. Jamestown, the settlement that almost failed, grew and prospered.

JAMESTOWN

Unsettled Wilderness

1607
Jamestown
is founded

THINGS TO DO

1. Make a diorama of one of the early Spanish missions. (A diorama is a scene in a box.) On the back of your box, paint a background for a mission scene. On the floor of the box, show a mission or some of the work that is done about the mission.

2. Pretend that you are the king's messenger carrying mail over *El Camino Real.* Write a short story telling what you saw as your horse galloped through the new settlements. Tell about the Indians you saw along the way. Tell about the *rancheros* on their farms and the priests at the missions.

3. Read more about the lives of the habitants of New France. Tell the class the most interesting things you read.

4. In another book, read the story about Captain John Smith and the Indian princess named Pocahontas. Tell the story to the class.

5. Make a diary that might have been kept by one of the settlers of Jamestown. In the diary write some of the experiences he might have had.

6. Start a class time line that will show how our country was settled. Begin your time line with the first French, Spanish, and English settlements.

LET'S TALK ABOUT —

1. Why it was hard for settlers to build homes in the New World.
2. How the Spanish, French, and English colonies differed.
3. Why the habitants were better settlers than the fur traders.
4. Why the Spaniards settled in the southern part of our country.
5. What lesson we can all learn from the settlers of Jamestown.
6. Why the early settlers were important to us.

A WORD GAME

The words below are used in the next story. Each of the words has a phrase that explains it. Can you find the phrase that belongs to each word?

purify	a large farm in the south
surrender	the members of a church
treaty	to give up
indigo	an agreement
plantation	a plant from which dye is made
congregation	to make pure, clean, or clear

There may be other words you will also want to put in your word file. If there are, explain the words to the class before you put them in your file.

NAMES YOU WILL MEET IN THE NEXT STORY

Plymouth	Squanto	Puritans	Peter Stuyvesant
Quakers	James Oglethorpe	Pilgrims	Mayflower Compact

Before You Read the Story —

When our country was being settled, England established thirteen colonies on the Atlantic seacoast. These thirteen colonies were the real beginnings of the United States.

You have already read how Virginia was settled. In this story you will read how the other twelve colonies were settled. The people who settled them were called colonists.

The colonists left England and came to America for different reasons. After you have read this story, talk about the reasons each group of colonists came to this country. Talk about the courage it took to face the dangers of a new, unsettled land. Talk about how difficult it was to build homes in a new country.

THIRTEEN
ENGLISH COLONIES

THE PILGRIMS COME TO AMERICA

In a little town in England a group of people had gathered in their meeting place. It was not a large church, nor a beautiful one. It was a secret chapel in a small but well-kept manor house.

As the meeting came to order the leader spoke. His voice was low. "We have met this morning," he said earnestly, "to plan a way of escape. We can no longer live in England. The Established Church is not our church, yet we are forced to belong to it. We are forced to pay taxes to support it.

"We have wandered many places seeking the right to worship in our own way. Each of our secret meeting places has been discovered. Some of us have been put in prison. Others have had their houses watched night and day. We do not wish to leave England, but we must be *free to worship God in our own way*."

In two years, more than one hundred men, women, and children had managed to escape into Holland. But the Pilgrims did not like Holland. When their children began to speak the Dutch language, they decided they must move again. *But where?* Finally they decided they would go to the New World. They joined Pilgrims from England and on August 5, 1620, two ships set sail for the New World. After two trials one ship could not go on.

One hundred two Pilgrims crowded on board the remaining ship, the *Mayflower*. On September 6, 1620, the *Mayflower* sailed from the harbor of Plymouth, England, to make the journey to America.

The trip across the Atlantic was stormy. For days and weeks the little ship tossed about in the rough sea. Many of the people became sick. Often they went hungry. Sometimes it seemed as if the voyage would never end!

The Pilgrims had been given permission to settle near Virginia. But the wind blew them northward. They finally pulled into Cape Cod Harbor, which is now Provincetown, Massachusetts. While they were in the harbor, the leaders called all the men into the cabin of the *Mayflower*.

"We do not have permission to settle here," said the leaders. "We do not have the government we expected to have in Virginia. We must plan a new government."

The men drew up a compact, or an agreement. In the compact they agreed to make just laws and to abide by the will of the majority. The compact was called *The Mayflower Compact*.

After the Compact was signed, the men tried to find a place for a settlement. On December 21, 1620, an exploring party of twelve men rowed into Plymouth Harbor looking for a place to land.

Finally they came to a large rock which they called Plymouth Rock. They chose the land around it for their settlement. They named their settlement Plymouth.

The Pilgrims landed at Plymouth Rock in the midst of winter. The long journey across the Atlantic had left many of them sick and weak. During the cold nights they slept on the *Mayflower*. In the daytime they chopped down the tall trees of the forest. They made houses, a fort, beds, tables, and chairs from the rough lumber.

In January and February nearly half of the little band died—sometimes two or three a day. At one time there were only six or seven well people in the whole colony.

During those dark days the well people went among the sick. They made fires, prepared food, made beds, and washed clothes. They did not grumble nor complain. They worked cheerfully and willingly.

In the spring a tall Indian walked down the streets of the little colony. He stopped at a house and said, "Welcome!" The colonists were surprised but very happy. The Indian told them his name was Samoset and that he had learned to speak English from the fishermen. He promised to come back and bring another Indian with him.

He brought an Indian named Squanto, who had lived in England. Squanto liked the white men. Before long he came to live in the Pilgrim settlement. He showed the colonists how to plant crops, where to catch fish, and where to hunt wild game.

During that first summer the Pilgrims worked long and hard. In the fall their harvest was bountiful. There would not be another winter of starving! The Pilgrims were so grateful that a time of thanksgiving was appointed.

The women prepared a great feast, which they served on long tables under the trees. The colonists invited the Indians to come and eat with them. For three days the Indians and the colonists feasted together. Then the Pilgrims gave thanks to God for their many blessings. *This was our first Thanksgiving Day.*

The Pilgrims had many hard times learning to live in America. But they had great courage. They had hearts willing to suffer hardships. They had hands ready to work. They helped to prepare the way for other colonists who came after them.

In 1620 the *Mayflower* sailed to the New World. On board were Pilgrims going to America to seek freedom of worship.

Before the men landed they all signed the *Mayflower* Compact. The Compact said the men would make and obey laws for their colony.

Even though it was winter, the Pilgrims began to build homes. But it was an unhappy time. Many of the people became sick and died.

In the spring an Indian named S q u a n t o showed the Pilgrims how to till the soil and plant crops that grew well in America.

When fall came, the harvest was bountiful. The Pilgrims invited the Indians to help them celebrate our first Thanksgiving Day.

On the edge of an unsettled wilderness, the Pilgrims had braved great hardships to establish the little Plymouth Colony.

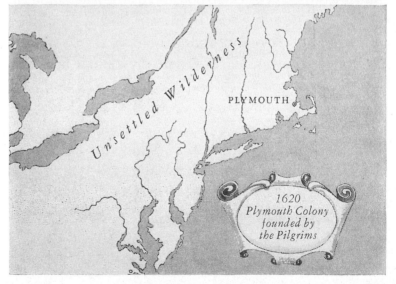

The Pilgrims left England because they did not believe in the teachings of the Church of England. Another group of people in England did not like the Church either. They wished to change, or to "purify," some of its teachings. For this reason they were called Puritans.

The Puritans were treated very cruelly in England. When they did not receive the same privileges as other Englishmen, they became more and more unhappy. Finally a plan to send them to the New World was worked out.

A group of merchants in England formed a company called the *Massachusetts Bay Company*. They bought or obtained land in America from the King. Then they gave the land and provided the money for the Puritans and other settlers to go to the New World. In return, they hoped to make money by trading with the colonists.

As soon as the Puritans decided to go to America, they obtained a charter, or permit, from the King. The charter allowed them to make their own laws and to elect their own officers. The charter also said they must obey the laws of England. But the Puritans knew in their hearts they would not obey the laws about religion.

There was one very strange thing about the charter given to the Puritans. Nearly every company or group of colonists that came to the New World was given a charter, but the charter was kept in England. *The Puritans were allowed to take their charter with them!*

Eight years after the Pilgrims landed at Plymouth Rock, a small party of Puritans sailed from England. They landed and established a colony at Salem, Massachusetts, not many miles from where the Pilgrims made their home.

Two years later a larger group of Puritans sailed to

America. In this group were eleven ships and about seven hundred settlers. They established the town of Boston.

Most of the Puritans who came to Boston were well to do. They brought many of their possessions with them. The men brought cows, horses, goats, tools, nails, window glass, locks, and other supplies. The women brought dishes, pots and pans, linens, and other things to make their homes more cheerful and more comfortable.

During the first few months in Boston many of the Puritans were sick. A large number of them died. But the others soon learned to live in their new home and the Massachusetts Bay Colony grew rapidly. As time went by, thousands of Puritans came over from England. Whole congregations, led by their pastors, sailed to America. They started new towns and villages.

In 1691, the weaker Pilgrim colony united with the Puritan colonies. The combined colony was then called *Massachusetts*.

When the Puritans left England, they decided to establish a colony for Puritans only. They could not do this, but they made it difficult for other people to live there. Only members of the church could vote or hold office. The Puritan leaders who held office were very religious. They made many strict and harsh laws.

They would not allow people to wear gay clothes, to play cards, or to celebrate Christmas. If anyone broke the law, he was punished severely. Cutting off an ear, burning with a hot iron, whipping, and putting a person in the stocks were common forms of punishment.

The Puritans left England because they did not like the Established Church of England. Yet they wanted everyone who came to their colony to join their church and to believe as they did!

The Puritans did not like the Church of England. They decided to go to the New World so they could worship as they chose.

The Puritans obtained permission to settle in America. They also got a charter that allowed them to govern themselves.

Many Puritans brought household goods with them to America. The men also brought cows, horses, tools, nails, and supplies.

The people soon learned to live in America. The men made rough lumber from the trees in the forest and built comfortable homes.

They plowed the soil and planted crops. More and more people went there to live. The colony prospered and grew rapidly.

The Puritans came to the New World in 1630. In 1691 the Pilgrim and the Puritan colonies united and became Massachusetts.

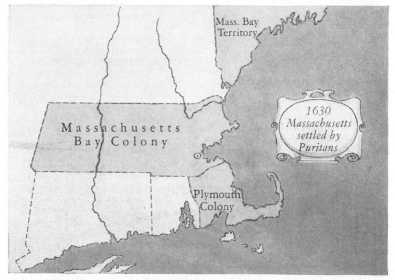

Mass. Bay Territory

Massachusetts Bay Colony

1630 Massachusetts settled by Puritans

Plymouth Colony

Roger Williams was a young Englishman who believed that everyone should have the right to worship God in his own way. "The King has no right to force any man to attend the Church of England," he declared. "Each man should have the right to worship God in any way he chooses." But he spoke too freely. He soon realized that he had to leave England or be put in prison.

Williams went from England to Massachusetts. There he received a warm welcome. But the welcome did not last long! Williams disagreed with many of the teachings of the Puritans.

He did not believe the church should be a part of the government. He did not believe in laws that forced the people to accept the beliefs of the Puritans. He did not believe the colonists should take land from the Indians without paying for it. He stated openly that the King did not have the right to grant land in America to anyone.

When the Puritan leaders heard the things Williams was preaching, they were very angry. They tried him in a court of law and sentenced him to leave the colony. Later they decided to send him back to England.

Williams heard what the leaders were planning to do. He did not want to return to England. "My task is here," he said. "When I first came to Massachusetts, I was very friendly with the Indians. I learned their language. I spent many hours in their wigwams teaching them about the Christian religion. I must stay with them and help them. I must also help the other colonists who believe as I do."

The night was dark and very cold. Roger Williams was ill. But he got out of bed and went out into the night alone. A snowstorm was raging. The sick man struggled on and on—through drifting snows and biting winds. Finally he stumbled into the camp of his Indian friends.

The Indians welcomed him and gave him food and shelter. They took care of him until he was well. In the spring, other colonists joined him. They started out to find a place for a new colony.

The spot they chose was part of what is now Providence, Rhode Island. For a long time Williams had dreamed of starting a colony where he could establish justice and freedom for all. He and his leaders planned that form of government for the new colony.

Before long, other people who did not like the stern rule of the Puritans came to Rhode Island. More towns were settled. The little colony, based on equal rights for all men, grew **and** prospered.

Roger Williams came to America to seek religious freedom. But the Puritans did not share his ideas of freedom.

Williams made friends with the Indians. He went among the various tribes and taught the Indians about the Christian religion.

The Puritan leaders did not like the way Williams was teaching. They finally decided to send him back to England.

Williams was ill when he heard what the leaders were planning. He got out of bed and went out into the storm to escape.

He struggled on until he came to some friendly Indians. The Indians took care of him until he was well again.

In the spring Williams and some of his friends went to look for a new place to live. They began the colony of Rhode Island.

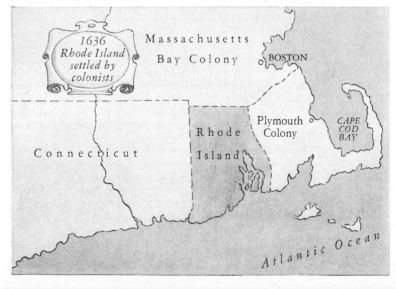

1636 Rhode Island settled by colonists

Massachusetts Bay Colony

BOSTON

Connecticut

Rhode Island

Plymouth Colony

CAPE COD BAY

Atlantic Ocean

CONNECTICUT IS SETTLED

Thomas Hooker was a preacher in England who refused to accept the ways of the Established Church. He believed that all men should have the right to choose their own religion. He not only believed it—he began to preach it on the streets and in the churches of England.

The English officials were very angry. They commanded Hooker to appear in court.

Hooker did not wish to appear in court to answer the British charges. Quickly and quietly he fled to Holland. From there he sailed to Massachusetts. In Massachusetts, Hooker became pastor of a church in Newtowne. The settlement of Newtowne was very new when Hooker first went there. "Here is my chance to build a colony based on religious freedom," he thought. He did not realize that the Puritans did not allow religious freedom in their colony!

Before long the Puritan leaders called on Hooker. They told him he must preach the views and beliefs of the Puritans. Secretly, Hooker was very angry. "I do not like the stern laws of the Puritans," he said to himself. "I do not believe the government should be controlled by the Church. I believe that all men should be free to help govern the colony and to choose their own religion."

Hooker had the courage to preach the things he believed.

Other men believed as he did. They and their families joined his congregation. Before long, Hooker's congregation grew very large. Soon there was not enough land around Newtowne for all of them.

The men called on the Reverend Mr. Hooker. "There is not enough land for all of us," they said. "There is not enough pasture for our sheep and our cattle. We cannot make a living for our families. We want to remain in your church, but what can we do?"

Hooker thought for some time. Then he remembered the stories he had heard about Connecticut. "I have heard many stories about the fertile lands in Connecticut," he told the men. "It is said the lands there are better than they are here. Let us move to Connecticut. Let us build a town where all men will have an equal chance."

In the spring of 1636 Hooker was ready to leave. About one hundred men, women, and children went with him. They sent their household goods down the river by boat. Then they herded their cattle in front of them and started toward the west.

Mrs. Hooker was ill and had to be carried on a litter. Most of the other people walked. A few rode in covered wagons drawn by oxen. The little group could travel only about seven or eight miles a day.

During the daytime they traveled the rough trails and drove their cattle before them. At night they camped along the trail.

In about two weeks they came to a beautiful spot in the fertile Connecticut Valley. There they began the town of Hartford, Connecticut. The men were delighted with the rich, new land. Eagerly and with a will they set to work. They built homes and established a government that gave more freedom to all.

Thomas Hooker told his congregation that he believed that every man should have the right to worship God in his own way.

The Puritans did not like Hooker's ideas, but his congregation grew rapidly. Soon there was not enough good land for all.

Hooker thought about stories he had heard of new and fertile lands in Connecticut. "Let us go there and start a new colony," he said.

In 1636, Hooker and part of his congregation began the long journey. They traveled over rough trails made by the Indians.

It was a slow journey. During the weary day, they walked and drove the cattle before them. At night they camped along the trail.

In about two weeks they came to the fertile Connecticut Valley. They began the town of Hartford and the colony of Connecticut.

Massachusetts Bay Colony

BOSTON

Connecticut

Rhode Island

Plymouth Colony

Atlantic Ocean

Long Island Sound

NEW AMSTERDAM

1636 Connecticut is settled

The Dutch lands in America, *discovered by Henry Hudson*, were called New Netherland. The first settlers who lived there were Dutch colonists who wanted to trade with the Indians. The colonists bought Manhattan Island from the Indians for a few strings of cheap beads and some brightly colored ribbons. The beads and the ribbons were worth about twenty-four dollars. Manhattan Island is now the heart of New York City. At that time the small Dutch city was called New Amsterdam.

From the very beginning the Dutch colonies in New Netherland prospered. The fur trade was good. The rich soil made excellent farming land. The rivers were full of fish and in the forest were many game birds. The people were well fed and prosperous, but they were not happy under their form of government.

The colony was ruled by the Dutch West India Company. The company sent over one governor after another. Most of the governors were selfish men who cared little about the rights of the people. One of these governors was Peter Stuyvesant.

Stuyvesant had lost a leg in battle. He stumped about on a wooden peg with silver bands around it. A proud man, he wanted to have his way in all things. He would not let the people help to make their own laws and many of them began to dislike him.

Some of the colonists told Stuyvesant they wanted a government like the colonists had in New England. He promptly told them they should be "hanged on the tallest tree in the land."

At that time Holland and England were at war. The English had long wanted the rich fur trade in New Netherland. In 1664, four English ships were sent to conquer the Dutch and seize New Netherland. The ships were anchored in the harbor and the British guns were pointed toward the little city. The British commander sent Stuyvesant a letter telling him to surrender or the British guns would open fire. Stuyvesant tore the letter to bits!

Angrily he stumped back and forth. "I will never surrender," he shouted loudly. "I will *never* take down the Dutch flag." But the colony was not armed. It could not hold out against the British cannon, and the people were tired of Stuyvesant's rule. They forced him to surrender before even a shot was fired.

After Stuyvesant surrendered, the British changed the name of New Netherland to New York. They changed the name New Amsterdam to the City of New York. Under British rule, the little colony began to grow very rapidly. More and more settlers came over from Europe. Settlers from other colonies moved there, too. In a few years New York became a rich and prosperous colony.

Holland sent colonists to America to settle the land discovered by Henry Hudson. The colony was called New Netherland.

New Netherland was a rich colony. In 1664, Holland and England were at war. The English sent ships to capture New Netherland.

The captain of the ships sent a letter to Peter Stuyvesant, the governor of New Netherland. He told Stuyvesant he must surrender.

114

Stuyvesant tore up the letter. He stamped about, shouting angrily, "I will not surrender. New Netherland will never become English."

But the people disliked Stuyvesant. They made him surrender before the British fired a shot. The colony became British.

The British changed the name of New Netherland to New York. They changed the name of New Amsterdam to New York City.

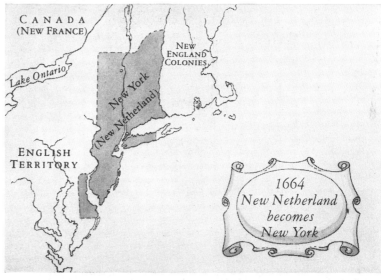

CANADA
(NEW FRANCE)

Lake Ontario

NEW ENGLAND COLONIES

New York
(New Netherland)

ENGLISH TERRITORY

1664
New Netherland
becomes
New York

"We want to worship God in our own way," said the unhappy people. "We cannot do so in England. Let us go to America, where we will be free. Let us establish a colony for Catholics. Better still, let us establish a colony where all people will have the right to worship as they choose." *Once more a colony was started in the New World because people wanted religious freedom.*

The Church of England was the only church recognized and protected by the King. But there were other churches and religions in England. The Catholic Church was one of the oldest and strongest, but even the Catholics were often punished because they did not believe in the Established Church.

George Calvert, or Lord Baltimore, was a devout Catholic who lived at that time. When he saw how cruelly the Catholics were treated in England, he dreamed of starting a colony where they would be free and happy. He also wanted to make his colony a place where other people could worship as they chose.

The King gave Lord Baltimore a large grant of land just north of Virginia. "What an excellent place for a colony," Lord Baltimore thought. But before he could send out a colony he died. His oldest son, Cecil, then

116

became Lord Baltimore. The second Lord Baltimore sent his brother Leonard to begin the colony planned by his father.

In 1634 Leonard Calvert sailed up the Potomac River with a group of settlers. The settlers were hard-working people who had studied how to live in the new country. They would not have the difficult times suffered by the men at Jamestown and the Pilgrims at Plymouth!

On the shores of a little stream that flowed into the Potomac, the settlers found a group of Indians who were planning to move. Calvert asked the Indians if they would sell their village. For a few yards of cloth, some hatchets, and some hoes, the Indians sold the settlers their land, their houses, their supplies of food, and their cleared fields.

The settlers named their new colony *Maryland* in honor of Queen Mary of England. The Catholic Church was the State Church, but other religions were welcomed, too.

From the very beginning, the colony of Maryland grew and prospered. Much of the soil was rich. The climate was milder than it was in some of the colonies to the north. The settlers soon found they could grow tobacco as well as other crops. In a few years many fertile fields were laid out along the wide rivers flowing into Chesapeake Bay.

Lord Baltimore was a devout Catholic. In England Catholics often were treated cruelly. Lord Baltimore thought about America.

"I would like to build a colony where all people can worship as they wish," he said. The King gave him some land in America.

Lord Baltimore died before he could start a colony. But his son Leonard took a party of colonists to the land north of Virginia.

The settlers found a group of Indians who were moving. The settlers bought the land from the Indians for a few trinkets.

The settlers soon learned to grow tobacco and other crops. From the very beginning, the little colony grew and prospered.

The colony was named Maryland in honor of Queen Mary. The Catholic Church was the State Church, although other churches were welcomed.

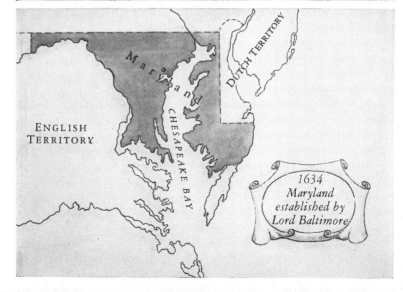

ENGLISH TERRITORY

DUTCH TERRITORY

Maryland

CHESAPEAKE BAY

1634
Maryland
established by
Lord Baltimore

It was a beautiful day in November, 1683. The Indians and the white men had met under the spreading branches of a giant oak tree. The Indians looked very gay in their bright-colored blankets, feathers, and beads. The white men were dressed in gray suits and broad, black hats.

After the two exchanged greetings, the Indians squatted down on the ground. The white men sat facing them. White curls of smoke puffed from the Indian pipe of peace as the chief lighted it. With great ceremony he smoked the pipe first, and then passed it slowly around the circle. Each man smoked it as his promise of peace.

Then the white man began to read from a piece of paper he held in his hand. "We will be brethren, my people and your people, as the children of one father. All the paths shall be open to the Christian and the Indian. . . . The Indian shall not harm the Christian nor his friend; the Christian shall not harm the Indian nor his friend; but they shall live together as brethren."

After reading the paper the white man began to talk. "We have come here to build homes for our families," he told the Indians. "You have much land. Will you sell some of your fields and your forests? What goods will you accept as money? Will you let us live in peace?"

The Englishmen opened big boxes they had brought with them. Out of the boxes came bright beads, knives, hatchets, cloth, and other trinkets loved by the red men. The Indians' eyes grew wide with delight. They reached for the things held out by the white men. As they did so, they nodded their heads. They had sold their land. The white men had bought and paid for it.

Then the leader of the white men pointed to the paper.

120

"The paper says that we agree to live in peace and to keep our promises," he told the Indian chief. The chief and the white man, *William Penn*, shook hands. This meant that they would both live by the agreement.

William Penn was a Quaker who lived in England. The Quakers, or Friends, did not believe in the Established Church. They believed that all men were equal before God. They would not take off their hats even to the King.

They were a peace-loving people, but they found little peace in England. They were treated so cruelly they wanted to leave and find new homes.

Penn's father had been a very rich man. When he died, the King owed him a large sum of money. William went to the King and suggested that he pay back the debt in land. The King had many acres of land in America. He was very happy to pay his debt by giving Penn a large region of land in America. The land was called *Pennsylvania*, which means "Penn's Woods."

Although the King gave Penn the land, the Quakers also *bought* it from the Indians. They made treaties with the red men and treated them as brothers. At first most of the settlers in Pennsylvania were Quakers. But it was not long before people came there from many lands. They were all treated fairly and the Quaker colony grew and became one of the largest of the English colonies.

William Penn laid out the city of Philadelphia on the banks of the Delaware River. Philadelphia means "city of brotherly love." The city was mapped out in square blocks, far different from the crooked, winding streets of English cities.

Penn was soon called back to England. But even then he watched over his colony in America. He helped many people find religious freedom and get a new start in life.

In England the people who believed in the Quaker religion were treated very cruelly. William Penn was a Quaker leader.

When Penn's father died the King owed him a large sum of money. Penn suggested the King pay the debt with land in America.

The King gave Penn a large tract of land in America. The land was called Pennsylvania. Penn took a group of settlers there.

The King gave Penn the land, but the Quakers also bought it from the Indians. They treated the Indians as their brothers.

William Penn laid out the city of Philadelphia on the banks of the Delaware River. Philadelphia means "brotherly love."

The Quakers were fair to everyone. Many people went to Pennsylvania. They all found religious freedom and a new start in life.

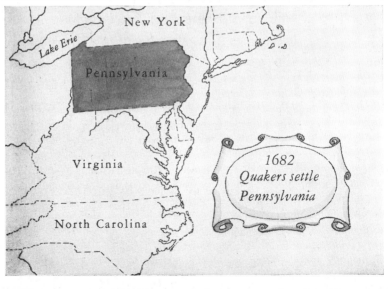

1682
Quakers settle
Pennsylvania

In 1663 the King of England gave eight of his friends the land between Florida and Virginia. In 1670 a party of settlers built a village there which they called Charlestown. The city was later moved and is now Charleston, South Carolina.

The owners of the land wished to make money by trading with the Indians, by renting the land to the settlers, or by selling lumber. But the owners and the settlers could not agree. Finally the owners sold the land back to the King. The King divided the land into two colonies, North Carolina and South Carolina. He appointed governors to rule over them.

In the Carolinas the soil was fertile, the climate warm. It was a good place to raise tobacco, rice, and indigo.

Raising tobacco is a difficult task because most of the work is done by hand. The tiny tobacco seeds are first planted in small seed beds of earth that has been mixed with wood ashes. Then, when the plants are a few inches high, they are taken into the fields and planted in rows. In the fields the young plants are carefully watched so the worms do not injure them.

As the plants grow, the tops are cut off so the plant will spread out and grow better leaves. When the big leaves begin to turn yellow, the plant is cut off close to the ground. The harvested plants are then placed on racks to dry. When they are thoroughly dry, the leaves are pulled from the stalks and sorted. In the early days the leaves were packed in barrels and shipped to England.

The colonists who raised tobacco made a good living. Those who raised rice and indigo also made a good living.

Near some of the southern rivers were great stretches

of swampy land. A settler planted rice in one of the swamps. His neighbors laughed. "Rice will not grow in America!" they said. To everyone's surprise the rice plants grew. The man harvested a good crop. Soon there were many fields of rice in the warm, wet lands of the Carolinas.

The story of indigo is the story of a little girl. Eliza Lucas lived with her mother on a farm in South Carolina. One day her father, who was a British soldier, sent her a package. In the package were indigo plants from one of the islands. "I doubt if the plants will grow," her father's letter said. But Eliza planted them.

The indigo plants grew tall and strong. Eliza was very proud of them. When her father heard that the plants were growing, he sent a man to show the people how to make indigo dye.

The man cut the plants, soaked them in water, and beat them with a stout stick. As the plants decayed, the water became deeply colored. The colored water was treated and allowed to settle. The indigo sank to the bottom as mud. The indigo mud made an excellent blue dye.

The clothmakers in England were very happy that indigo could be grown in America. They paid well for the dye, and the raising of indigo became an important industry in the Carolinas.

The indigo, rice, and tobacco plantations were very large. The work on them was not easy. The tobacco plants had to be watched very carefully. The swampy rice lands were hot, as well as wet.

The colonists soon found that colored people could stand the work in the fields much better than white men. More and more Negro slaves were brought over from Africa. Before long most of the work on the southern plantations was done by Negroes.

In 1663, the King gave some of his friends the land between Florida and Virginia. In 1670, the owners sent settlers there.

The settlers built a little town and called it Charlestown. They raised tobacco and sent great barrels of it to England.

The settlers and the owners made money. But it was hard to work in the hot fields of the South. Soon Negroes were brought there.

Negroes did the heavy work in the fields. They planted and harvested rice, tobacco, and indigo. The farms became plantations.

But the owners and settlers could not agree. Both thought the other unfair. Finally the owners sold the land back to the King.

The King divided the land into two colonies. He called them North and South Carolina. He appointed governors to rule them.

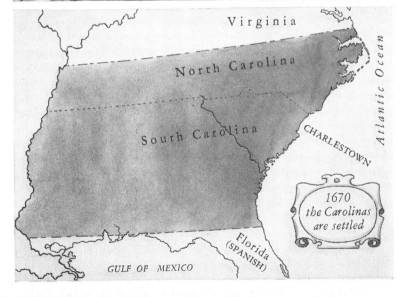

1670
the Carolinas
are settled

NEW HAMPSHIRE BECOMES A SEPARATE COLONY

New Hampshire had a strange beginning. When most of the colonies were founded, they were given charters by the King of England. New Hampshire did not receive a royal charter! It was started in a very different way.

In 1620 Sir Ferdinando Gorges and some of his friends formed a group called the Council for New England. They asked the King to give them land in America. The King granted them the land that is now New England.

The Council divided the land into several parts. It gave some of the land to Captain John Mason and some to Gorges. Mason named his grant New Hampshire in honor of his old home in England. The land that was given to Gorges is now part of the state of Maine.

One piece of land was given to Mason and Gorges together. After a few years they divided it. Mason added his share to New Hampshire. Still later the Council decided to give more land to Mason. This he also added to New Hampshire. *New Hampshire, unlike any other colony, was founded piece by piece!*

Both Gorges and Mason tried to establish colonies on their land. They wanted to make money by trading with the Indians. But the colonies were not successful.

After the colonies failed, the Puritans from Massachusetts began to move into the territory. Immediately there was trouble. Mason and Gorges said that the territory belonged to them. The Massachusetts Bay Colony claimed the land had been given to them in their grant from the King. The dispute lasted for many years.

Finally, in 1679, the King made New Hampshire a separate colony. Maine remained a part of Massachusetts until 1820.

NEW JERSEY AND DELAWARE BECOME COLONIES

The colonists in New Jersey did not have a "starving time" as did the settlers in Virginia. They did not have the unhappy time suffered by the Pilgrims. The early story of New Jersey is more like a game of ball. First "one side" had the land—then the other. For a time it seemed as if two countries "took turns" ruling the territory.

After Henry Hudson visited the New World, *Dutch* traders settled in New Jersey. Then colonists from *Sweden* came there, too. The Dutch forced the Swedish colonists to surrender to Holland. A little later the Dutch, themselves, were forced to surrender to the *English*.

England gave the land the name of New Jersey. But the English rule did not last long. A few years later Holland recaptured the land. This did not last long, either. The next year England took back New Jersey! But this time the "game" was over—England kept the land and settled it.

England divided the territory into two parts—East Jersey and West Jersey. *In 1702 the two Jerseys joined and formed the permanent colony of New Jersey.*

The story of Delaware is much the same as the story of New Jersey. It, too, is the story of many people and many governments. The *Dutch* settled there first. Then *Swedish* colonists moved in. The Swedish colonists surrendered to the Dutch. Then the Dutch surrendered to the English. The Dutch recaptured Delaware. But finally England took the land and kept it.

Later the King gave part of Delaware to William Penn. Penn made the territory part of Pennsylvania. But the people of Delaware did not like this. Finally tiny Delaware pulled away and became an independent colony.

Captain John Mason and Sir Ferdinando Gorges tried to start colonies in Maine and New Hampshire. They were not successful.

When the colonies failed, the Puritans began to move into the territory. Mason, Gorges, and the Puritans all claimed the territory.

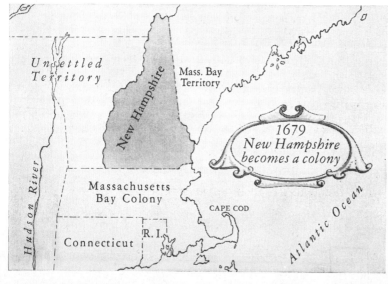

Unsettled Territory

Mass. Bay Territory

New Hampshire

1679 New Hampshire becomes a colony

Hudson River

Massachusetts Bay Colony

CAPE COD

R. I.

Connecticut

Atlantic Ocean

Finally, in 1679, the King declared New Hampshire a separate colony. Maine remained part of Massachusetts until 1820.

The Dutch, the Swedish, and the English settled in New Jersey and Delaware. All of these countries fought to govern the colonies.

At last England captured New Jersey and managed to keep it. The permanent colony of New Jersey was established in the year 1702.

England also captured Delaware and made it part of Pennsylvania. But the colonists pulled away to form the colony of Delaware.

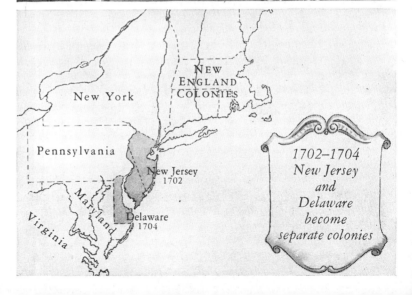

New York

NEW ENGLAND COLONIES

Pennsylvania

New Jersey 1702

Maryland

Virginia

Delaware 1704

1702–1704
New Jersey
and
Delaware
become
separate colonies

The men at Jamestown began the first English colony in the New World in 1607. It was more than a hundred years later before the last English colony was planted in America. It seems strange, but *Georgia*, the last colony, was chartered the year George Washington was born.

Some of the men who planned to build colonies in America wanted to make money. James Oglethorpe, the man who founded Georgia, did not think only of himself. He thought of poor men who needed a new start in life. For this reason there was a different motto on the charter that the King gave him. It was a Latin motto which meant "Not for self but for others."

Oglethorpe had once served in the British army. When he retired, he became interested in the government. At that time anyone in England who could not pay his debts was thrown into prison. Oglethorpe had a friend who died in a debtors' prison. The man died because he was not given good food nor good care.

Oglethorpe immediately became interested in the English prisons. He found that conditions were very poor. The rooms in the prisons were small and dark. Prisoners were crowded together with very little air in their cells. Many of them were sick. Dirt and filth covered everything.

Oglethorpe felt sorry for the people in prison. He did not believe that a man should be kept in jail merely because he could not pay his debts. He went to the King and asked for a grant of land in America. He asked to start a colony where the people in prison and other unhappy people could begin new and useful lives.

The King gave him land in the southern part of South Carolina. This land was close to Spanish Florida and

132

had never been settled by white men. The Spaniards and the Indians had often attacked the settlers in South Carolina. The people in South Carolina were happy to have an English colony to the south. They felt it would protect them from attack.

The English government freed some of the prisoners and gave Oglethorpe a large sum of money to start the new colony. Religious groups also promised to give money if he would build schools and churches for the Indians.

In 1733 Oglethorpe led a group of settlers to America. Most of the men had been in prison. They and their families were glad to start life anew. They built the town that is now Savannah, Georgia.

For a number of years Oglethorpe governed Georgia. He knew that Spain would try to destroy the little colony, but he was prepared. His colonists and friendly Indians fought back against attacks by the Spaniards. The colonists won their battles and finally Georgia was secure. Then Oglethorpe went back to England.

The colony of Georgia grew very slowly. But England now had colonies along the Atlantic seacoast from Spanish Florida to French Canada.

The Thirteen Colonies. Thirteen English colonies had been established in the New World. These thirteen colonies were to become the United States of America. Most of the colonists had come to America in search of freedom. They wanted to live their lives in their own way!

Hunger, sickness, and suffering did not change their hearts nor their minds. No matter how many hardships they endured, they still wanted to be free. Later they proved to the world that they not only wanted freedom, but they were willing to *fight* for it.

133

In early times any Englishman who could not pay his debts was put into prison. James Oglethorpe felt sorry for the men in prison.

He asked the King for land in America. He wanted to begin a colony where the men in the prisons could start life anew.

The King gave him land in the southern part of Carolina, and freed some of the prisoners. Oglethorpe led a party to the New World.

134

Most of the men had been in prison. Others had been in trouble. They and their families were glad to start a new life in America.

The first settlement in the colony was at Savannah. The town was laid out by Oglethorpe, and the men built their houses there.

Oglethorpe governed the colony for nine years. Then he went back to England. *The last English colony had been settled.*

Unsettled lands deeded to colonies (also claimed by France)

North Carolina

South Carolina

Georgia

SAVANNAH

Florida (SPANISH)

1733
Georgia
is settled

THINGS TO DO

1. Pretend you were the captain of the *Mayflower*. Write a log of the journey across the Atlantic. (A log is a record the captain of a ship keeps of each sea voyage.) In your log of the *Mayflower,* write down the things you think might have happened on board ship.

2. Talk about why the signing of the Mayflower Compact was important to us. Act out the signing of the Compact.

3. Make a class "picture" map that will show *why, how, when,* and *where* the thirteen colonies were established.

4. Divide the class into thirteen sections. Let each section choose one of the thirteen colonies. Read more about how the colony was established. Report to your own group first; then make a report to the class.

5. Finish your time line of colonization. Compare it with your time line of exploration.

LET'S TALK ABOUT—

1. Why the Pilgrims had a more difficult time building homes in the New World than the Puritans had.

2. How the Pilgrims helped to make it easier for the other colonists to build homes.

3. The reasons the different colonists came to America.

4. Why it took as much courage to build homes in the New World as it did to explore the country.

5. How the desire for freedom led people to the New World.

6. How the colonists helped us to enjoy the many things that we have today.

136

NEW WORDS

The following words are used in the next story. They may be new to you. If they are, look up their meanings in your dictionary. Write sentences using these words. Put the new words in your word file.

basque	thatched	gourd	gallery
sapling	trencher	wampum	pillars
stockade	bayberry	attached	swingle
lye	fibers	misbehaved	pewter
	treadle	pillory	

Before You Read the Story—

The Pilgrims and the men at Jamestown suffered greater hardships than the other colonists. They were the first English people to build homes in the New World. They did not bring with them as many supplies as the later colonists brought. They had no place to turn for help. During their first winter in America they suffered greatly from cold, hunger, and sickness.

But the colonists soon learned to live in the new land. As the years passed, life in the colonies changed rapidly. The times of starving were over. The first crude houses were replaced with better houses built of lumber or brick. The people did not have some of the comforts they had known in the Old World, but life was pleasant.

After you have read this story, talk about how ways of living changed in colonial times. Talk about how the people in the different colonies lived. Talk about how colonial ways of living were very different from the way that we live today.

WORK AND PLAY
IN THE COLONIES

LIFE IN EARLY AMERICA

Chains rattled as the *Mayflower* dropped anchor in Plymouth Harbor. The ship had landed on the coast of Cape Cod a few weeks before, but the Pilgrims had decided to go on. Now they felt that their journey was really over. How good it was to see land! How good it was to see the tall trees of the forest! Surely in this wooded land they could find a place to build homes.

The children crowded around the railing of the ship. They laughed and chattered merrily. What an exciting place the new land was! They could not understand why their parents looked worried. They could not understand why the men sometimes talked in low, strained voices.

The Pilgrim children were dressed much as their parents were dressed. The girls wore long, full skirts with tight basque waists. On their heads they wore stiff white caps. The boys wore short trousers, long jackets, and broad-brimmed hats. Most of the Pilgrims wore dark clothes. The dark clothes meant less washing for the women.

After the ship was anchored, some of the men rowed ashore in a longboat. Before many hours they came back. "We found good soil, but not fresh water," they said. "We must look still farther for a place to build our homes."

The next day was the Sabbath. There was no work done on that day. To the Pilgrims, it was a day of prayer.

139

Men, women, and children joined in giving thanks that they had arrived safely in the New World. They asked God to help them in finding a place to build a settlement.

When Monday morning dawned, the women began to bustle about the ship. It was now their turn to go on shore. They wanted to wash their clothes before a storm came. The longboat was loaded with kettles, tubs, and dirty clothes. Then the women were taken ashore.

What a busy time it was! Fires were built along the shore, and water from the ocean was heated for washing. When the water was hot, the clothes were put into the big tubs. How the women rubbed and scrubbed! When the clothes were clean, they were hung on bushes to dry. It was a hard day's work for the women. But how good it was to smell the fresh, clean clothes!

Each day the men looked for a place to build a settlement. It was nearly a month before they found one. Then they found some fields that had been cleared and left by the Indians. Not far from the fields was a little stream of water that emptied into Plymouth Bay. The Pilgrims named the stream the Jones River in honor of the captain of the *Mayflower*. A few days before Christmas they went ashore to build their colony along the river.

In icy winds, in snow and sleet, the men began to cut down the trees of the forest. From early morning until late at night they worked. The white chips flew as their sharp axes sank deep into the big trees. Sometimes the chips were covered with falling snowflakes. Sometimes the hands of the men were blue with cold as they sawed the big logs into rough, uneven boards.

The Pilgrims first built a large house, which they called the *common house*. The sides of the common house were made of rough boards. The cracks between the boards were

140

filled with twigs and clay. The roof of the house was made of bundles of grass fastened together. This kind of roof is called a thatched roof and was made very steep so the rain and snow would fall off.

After the common house was built, some of the Pilgrims went there to live. The others stayed on board the *Mayflower* until more houses could be built.

Each family was supposed to build its own house, but that first winter the work went slowly. Nearly all the people were sick and many of them died. Then came the first warm days of spring. The discouraged Pilgrims found new hope. More cabins were built, the land was plowed, and crops were planted. Before long the women began to sing as they went about their work.

Most of the early Pilgrim cabins had one large room where the family lived, ate, and slept. The windows and doors in the cabins were rough boards held together with wooden pegs or strips of leather. When they were closed, the only light in the cabin was the light that strayed down through the opening in the fireplace.

The furniture in the room was made by the men and boys. The chairs were rough stools without backs, and the tables were long boards placed on wooden legs. The beds were rough boards tied together with rope or strips of leather. The mattresses were filled with straw.

Sometimes the people longed for the comforts of their homes in the Old World. But they had little time to dream! There was *work* to be done if the New World were to become a good place in which to live.

It was not easy to change from life in the Old World to life in the New. But if a boy from England could have visited the early colonists in America, he might have kept a diary much like this:

I arrived safely at the home of my British cousins in America. Sometimes I wonder how they can like this strange, lonely land! Today Richard, my eldest cousin, took me to visit some of his friends near Boston. They live in wigwams made from hickory saplings. The men had cut the green saplings and had sharpened them at one end. Then they had driven them into the ground like stakes.

The green saplings will bend without breaking. The men had bent the saplings and tied them together at the top to make a rounded roof. Then they had covered the roof with woven mats. On top of the mats they had laid pine bark like shingles to make the wigwam snug and warm.

The wigwams are strange places to live, but some of the people even live in dugout houses until they can build their cabins. The dugout houses are like little caves dug in the side of a hill or the bank of a river. There are doors on the outside of the dugout, and the chimney from the fireplace rises above the ground.

— Tuesday

When we returned from Boston, Aunt Mary was preparing supper. The stew was bubbling and boiling in the big iron kettle that hung over the fireplace. The boys were pulling wooden benches around the long table. The girls were putting wooden trenchers on the table.

A trencher is a block of wood ten or twelve inches square and three or four inches deep. It is hollowed out into a sort of bowl. Robert and I used the same trencher. We ate our stew with pewter spoons.

After supper was over and the kitchen was cleared, Uncle Henry told Robert to light a pine knot. The pine knot burned with a bright, smoky flame. It looked like a torch, but it gave a good light. Uncle Henry took down the

142

family Bible and sat in a chair by the fireplace. The family gathered around him.

In a clear voice he read a chapter from the Bible. Then we all said prayers and went to bed. Robert and I climbed the ladder to the loft over the kitchen. It was cold, and we pulled off our boots quickly. The straw mattress rustled as we piled into bed. But we were soon asleep.

— *Wednesday*

Uncle Henry called us this morning as soon as it was light. During the night the snow had drifted through the cracks between the rough boards. Richard shook the snow off our coverlet and we jumped out of bed. We had slept in our clothes, so we pulled on our boots and climbed down the ladder into the kitchen.

143

Before breakfast we had long prayers. Then we ate corn-meal mush and milk. After breakfast Uncle Henry went hunting in the forest. We walked with him as far as the gate in the tall stockade.

The stockade is a high post fence built to protect the settlers from the Indians. Most of the Indians are friendly and help the colonists. But some of them are warlike, and the settlers want to be prepared. They have built a fort in the stockade and on top of the hill they have placed guns and a cannon.

— *Thursday morning*

As I write, I am looking about the cabin. In one corner is a large spinning wheel for spinning wool. Near it is a smaller wheel for spinning flax. Over the fireplace are cow-horns filled with powder and shot, and a long rifle.

Hanging from chains in the fireplace are big kettles. All the pots and kettles have three legs so that hot coals can be put under them as they stand before the fire.

Near the fireplace are long-handled forks and a shovel. The shovel is used to lift hot food from the oven. Aunt Mary has a stone oven built at one side of her fireplace. She is fortunate because few women have ovens.

From the ceiling of the cabin hang strips of dried apples, onions, and cobs of corn. For special dinners Aunt Mary soaks the apples in water. Then she cooks them with wild honey the boys have gathered in the forest.

Most of the time we use pine torches for light, but Aunt Mary has two Betty lamps and some candles. A Betty lamp is like a shallow iron dish with a spout at one end. The wick hangs from the spout but the rest of the lamp is covered over. Fish oil, lard, animal fat, and whale oil are burned in the lamps. The lamps give a fair light, but they are smoky. I like the candlelight best.

144

Aunt Mary has a large "soap barrel" which she keeps in the shed. Every bit of fat and leftover grease goes into the barrel. Not even a tiny scrap is thrown away! This afternoon the barrel was full. Aunt Mary decided it was time for soapmaking.

We hung a big black kettle in the back yard. In the kettle we put the scraps of fat and some lye. Underneath the kettle we built a roaring fire. In a little while the lye and the fat were bubbling merrily.

We took turns watching the soap and gathering wood to keep the fire burning. After a while, the fat and lye had boiled down as thick as jelly. Then it was poured out into a barrel. When it cools it will become a soft soap that can be dipped out of the barrel with a large spoon. The soft soap is used for washing clothes and bathing.

Sometimes Aunt Mary saves the best pieces of fat and adds salt to the fat and lye. This makes a soap that will harden so it can be cut into blocks. In some of the hard soap, Aunt Mary puts perfume made from crushed leaves. She often gives this soap away for wedding and birthday presents.

— Friday afternoon

We dipped candles this morning. It was fun. The tallow for the dipping was put into a big iron kettle. While it was melting, we twisted cotton wicks and put them on candle rods. Then we dipped the wicks into the tallow.

We made a number of candles at the same time. When the last candle was dipped, the first one was cool enough to dip again. We dipped and cooled and dipped and cooled until the candles were the right size. Then we put them away to harden until they were ready to be used.

While we were dipping the tallow candles, Aunt Mary told me she also made bayberry candles. When the bayberry is ripe, it is coated with wax. The wax melts easily and rises to the top of the kettle when the berries are put into boiling water. Bayberry wax makes a harder candle than tallow and burns much longer. It is a delicate green and gives off a faint perfume when it burns.

— *Friday evening*

Aunt Mary and the older girls weave both woolen and linen cloth. They also make clothes from the skins of animals. The clothes are not so pretty as the clothes we wear in England, but they are warm and comfortable.

146

Not far from the house Uncle Henry has a field of flax. When the flax is ripe, the plants are pulled up and left in the sun to dry. While they are drying, the seed pods are taken off and the seeds are carefully saved. Then the flax is tied into bundles and put into water.

The water rots the green stalks and the leaves. When the rotted part drops off, the real work begins. Inside the stalks are tough fibers. The fibers must be separated from the stalks before they can be spun into thread.

To do this, the flax is put on the flax brake. It is crushed until only the tough, threadlike fibers are left. The fibers are then beaten with a swingle. The swingle removes any little pieces that still cling to the fibers. It also makes the fibers soft so they will bend easily.

The next step is called *hackling* the flax. The hackles are square pieces of wood set with wire teeth. The flax fibers are wet slightly and drawn through the hackle. The hackle combs out the short and brittle pieces, and leaves only the long fibers, which will make good thread. The long fibers are tied into bundles and left until the women and girls can spin them into thread.

I watched Elizabeth spin flax this evening. She sat down by the small spinning wheel and wet her fingers with water from a gourd. Then she picked up a few strands of flax and fastened the ends onto the spindle. With her foot she pressed the treadle of the spinning wheel. The spindle began to whirl around and around. As it turned, it twisted the flax into a hard, even thread.

When Elizabeth had finished, Richard put the thread away. He said Aunt Mary would bleach it and weave it into linen cloth. Then the cloth would be dyed with the juices of flowers, leaves, berries, or the bark from trees. The flax makes good linen clothes for summer.

147

The flax was cut, tied into bundles, and dried in the sun. Then it was soaked in water to rot the stalks and leaves.

Then the stalks were crushed on the flax brake until only the tough fibers were left. The fibers were beaten with a swingle.

The swingle left the fibers soft so they could be drawn through the hackle to comb out the short fibers and leave the long ones.

148

The long fibers were tied into bundles for spinning. As the spinning wheel turned, the strands of flax twisted into hard thread.

After the flax was spun into a hard, even thread, it was often bleached. Then it was woven into cloth on a homemade loom.

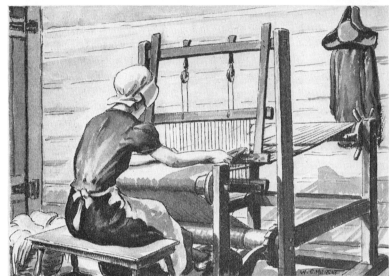

The finished cloth was dyed with the juices of flowers, wild berries, leaves, or bark from trees. The flax made a good linen cloth.

Today is Saturday and everyone in the family is busy. Richard is chopping enough wood to last until Monday morning. The girls are cooking, sewing, and cleaning. Uncle Henry is making a pair of shoes for Elizabeth to wear to church tomorrow. Aunt Mary is busy, too, but she took time to tell me how they make woolen cloth.

In the spring the sheep are sheared and the wool is rolled into big bundles ready to be sorted. When it is sorted, the coarse and dirty wool is put into one pile to be made into yarn for knitting. The fine white wool is put into another pile to be spun into yarn for weaving.

After the wool is sorted, it is carded. The cards are large wooden brushes with strong wire teeth. One card is put on the knee and bunches of matted wool are laid across the teeth. The other card is used as a comb.

The card that is used as a comb is drawn over the first card until the wool is straightened out. Then the wool is gathered into a soft roll for spinning.

I asked Aunt Mary to show me how to spin wool. She smiled and brought out the big spinning wheel and some wool. She did not sit down as Elizabeth had done when she spun the flax. She stood up and walked back and forth while she was spinning. Yarn that is used for knitting or for coarse cloth is spun only once. Wool used for fine cloth is spun twice and twisted into a hard, tight thread.

I am beginning to like the New World better. It does not seem so strange and lonely any more. Uncle Henry and his family work hard, but they have many good times. Perhaps, some day, I shall come to live here, too.

In early colonial times each family lived in its own little world. The people often helped one another, but they learned to depend upon themselves. Goods sent over from England cost a great deal of money. Very few families could afford to buy them. The settlers learned to get along on what they could raise or make in America. Nearly every family raised its own food, built its own home, and made its own clothes.

But as soon as the people had homes and enough to eat, they began to long for the things they had known in the Old World. The fine furniture from England would make their homes more pleasant and attractive. The lovely silks, satins, laces, and woolens would make beautiful clothes.

Before long the people began to ship goods over from the Old World. They began to improve the things they made in America. Little by little their ways of living began to change. Some of the things they did would seem strange to us, but they are interesting.

151

The colonists raised sheep, not only for food, but to obtain wool. The wool was made into cloth for warm, winter clothing.

In the spring the sheep were sheared. The coarse, dirty wool was put into one pile. The fine white wool was put into another.

Then the wool was carded. After it had been combed out, it was taken off the cards and rolled into a soft ball for spinning.

The coarse wool was spun into yarn for knitting. The fine wool was spun into yarn to be woven into cloth for making clothes.

After the wool was spun into thread, it was gathered into long skeins. Then the skeins were dyed in kettles and hung up to dry.

The skeins of wool were woven into strong, warm cloth. The colonial women were proud of the cloth as it came off the looms.

EARLY SCHOOLS

In one corner of the room sits a small boy on a high, four-legged stool. On his head is a pointed dunce cap. Not far from the boy in the dunce cap is another boy hanging on the wall by his clothing. Both boys look a little frightened and a little ashamed. They are pupils in a *dame school* in New England. They have misbehaved and the teacher is punishing them.

The dame schools were the first schools in the colonies. They were taught by women who were too frail to do the heavy work about the house. The *dame* was not paid with money but was given food and clothing for her work.

A little later a schoolmaster taught the older children. They went to his home or to the town hall. The schoolmaster taught them reading, spelling, and writing. He also taught "sums" to the boys.

Then *public* schools were started in the northern colonies. Any child could attend, but his parents had to pay for his schooling. The richer families paid the most. But each family was supposed to pay all it could afford.

154

Everyone worked to keep the schools open. The parents furnished the wood to keep the schoolhouses warm. The older pupils kept the schoolroom clean. They cut the wood, brought it into the schoolhouse, and kept the fire burning. They carried drinking water from a spring or a nearby well. The teacher was paid very little, and it was not often that he was paid with money. Sometimes the parents paid him with chickens, ducks, or eggs. Sometimes they gave him corn, wheat, or vegetables. Sometimes he received furs or Indian wampum.

School was held six days a week. It began at seven or eight in the morning and closed at four or five in the afternoon. Recess was from eleven until one. Even on Sunday the boys and girls had to study. On Monday the teacher tested them on the sermon they had heard in church.

The teachers were very strict and stern. A child might be whipped because he

made a mistake or misbehaved. If he whispered, he had to wear the whispering stick. The whispering stick was a block of wood with a cord attached to each end. The block was put into the child's mouth and the cords were tied tightly around his head. The block was very uncomfortable, and most of the pupils did not whisper again.

The colonial schoolrooms were dark and gloomy. The desks were long boards that rested on crude wooden legs. The seats were hard benches.

The younger children studied from a *hornbook*. The hornbook was a small board with a handle. On the board was fastened a page cut from a book. The page usually had the alphabet, a few letter combinations, and the Lord's Prayer printed on it. It was covered with a thin sheet of cowhorn to protect it from tearing or wearing out.

The older children in the New England colonies studied from the *New England Primer*. The primer was a book with the alphabet, some letter combinations, prayers, religious verses, and a few poems in it.

The older girls did not go to school. After they had learned to read the Bible, their parents thought they should stay at home and learn to cook and sew.

GOING TO CHURCH

To the northern colonists, Sunday was a day of rest and prayer. No one did any work on that day. The women were not even allowed to cook for their families.

But Saturday was quite different. On Saturday the mother and girls cooked enough food to last until Monday morning. They scrubbed the house, and made sure that everyone had clean clothes. The boys filled the wood box. They built fires in the yard and heated water for baths.

After supper everyone studied the Bible for an hour. Then father said, "Bath time." The boys brought in the big wooden tub. They set it in front of the fireplace and filled it with warm water. The girls put screens on all sides of the tub except the side next to the fire. Then everyone took turns rubbing and scrubbing. When the last bath was finished, it was time for bed.

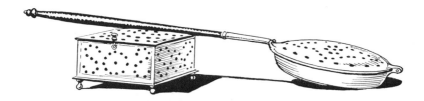

In the winter, the mother ran a *warming pan* between the bedcovers. The warming pan was a shallow copper dish with a long wooden handle. In the cover of the dish were little holes to let the heat escape. Before bedtime the pan was filled with live coals from the fireplace. Then it was run between the bedcovers to warm them.

On Sunday morning everyone went to church. In cold weather the people took *foot stoves* with them. The foot stoves were little iron boxes filled with glowing coals. They were put on the floor and used as footstools. They kept the feet warm, and warmed a little space in the room.

The meetinghouses were bare and uncomfortable. They were often divided into sections, and each family sat in its own pew. Sometimes the children sat in the gallery.

There was no organ in the church, but the people sang

the songs they had known in the Old World. Then the preacher began a long sermon. Sometimes the sermon lasted for more than two hours. The children became very restless. Even the grown people found it hard to keep awake!

The women were treated gently if they fell asleep. An usher brushed their faces with a feather, a rabbit's foot, or a foxtail until they awakened. The men and boys were not treated so gently. If a boy became sleepy or misbehaved in any way, an old man rapped him sharply on the head with a long stick.

EARLY FORMS OF PUNISHMENT

Nearly every colonial town had a whipping post. The lawbreaker was tied to the post and given blows on his bare back with a leather whip. Sometimes he even had his ears cut off or his tongue bored through with a hot iron.

A woman who scolded too much was put in the front yard with a gag in her mouth. She was also tied to the ducking stool and ducked in the water. If she complained, she was ducked again and again.

A man who did not attend church was put in the *stocks* or the *pillory*. The pillory was a rough board in which holes had been cut for the hands and the head. The board was fastened to a tall pole. The man was forced to stand with his head and his hands locked in the holes. It was neither pleasant nor comfortable to stand in the pillory. The next Sunday the man was usually in church!

The stocks were boards in which holes had been cut for the hands and the feet. Sometimes only the feet were fastened in the stocks. At other times both the hands and feet were locked tight. Near the stock or pillory was a sign that told which law had been broken.

The colonists soon found they had little time for amusement. But they knew that everyone must play as well as work. The people learned to combine their work with play. They often helped one another and finished the work with a picnic or a party.

When a family needed a new home, the neighbors came to help with the "house-raising." The men brought their axes and tools. They worked steadily until the framework of the house was finished. Then they had a party. Food prepared by the women was spread out on a long table. The happy group ate, laughed, and made merry.

Logrolling time was also fun. When a settler wanted to clear his land of logs, he invited his neighbors to come to a logrolling. To make the work seem more like play, the men divided themselves into two groups. The two groups raced to see which one could roll away the greatest number of logs.

When the last log was rolled away, the women and children joined the men. They ate, sang, and played games. The women helped one another,

too. When a colonial housewife needed quilts, she had a quilting bee. She invited her friends to come and help her make the soft, warm comforters. The women stitched, laughed, and chatted until the quilt was finished. Then the hostess served refreshments. To the women, the work seemed more like play!

During the crisp, cool days of autumn there were corn-husking and corn-shelling bees. The young people gathered out of doors or in the barn and husked and shelled the corn. When their work was finished, they played games or danced. The night air was often filled with the strains of lively music and the sound of merry laughter.

Sugar-making time was another happy occasion. In the northern colonies there were many fine maple groves. The sap from the maple trees was gathered in the early spring. Then it was put into big kettles and boiled until it became maple syrup or maple sugar. When the owner of the grove finished boiling the sap, the children waited eagerly. They knew there would be enough warm syrup in the bottom of the kettle for all!

The colonists worked hard but they enjoyed life in the New World. Whenever they could, they made their work fun.

LIFE ON A SOUTHERN PLANTATION

Through yellowed fields of ripe tobacco is a winding path. It begins at the little river dock where ocean vessels load tobacco. It leads through the fields, over wide green lawns, and to the door of a big white house.

On either side of the house are tall brick chimneys. Across the back of the house is a broad porch called a *veranda*. On both sides of the front door are beautiful pillars of carved wood.

In the front doorway of the house stands the wife of the plantation owner. She wears a silk dress with flowing sleeves and a long full skirt. Her ruffled dress is trimmed with laces and is worn over a hooped petticoat that makes the skirt stand out all around. On her head she wears a powdered wig brushed into many little curls. She looks beautiful and stately.

Beside the woman stand a boy and a girl. The boy's crimson-colored velvet jacket comes almost to his knees. It is trimmed with silver braid and large silver buttons.

162

The boy's short trousers fasten at the knee with silver buckles. His coat cuffs are turned back to show the white ruffles on his shirt. His waistcoat is made of embroidered satin. His shoes are decorated with jeweled buckles.

The girl is dressed much as her mother is dressed. Her pink satin dress comes to her ankles. Her velvet hood is trimmed with ruffled lace and satin ribbons.

The planter's wife and children are going to a party. Their everyday clothes are much plainer and are made of homespun linen, wool, or cotton cloth. Life on the plantation is pleasant, but there is still much work to be done.

From the veranda of his house, the planter can look out over his big plantation. In the distance, beyond the fields of rice and tobacco, is the river. A ship is being loaded with barrels of tobacco that are being sent to England. The planter smiles as he realizes that his crop will bring a high price, and in return he can buy many things from the English merchants.

Before the ship sails away, the planter gives the captain a list. The list names the things the planter and his family want from England. When the captain returns to pick up the planter's rice crop, he brings with him the things on the list. Perhaps he brings satin cloth, silk stockings, wigs, jewelry, and furniture.

The plantation is many miles from town and is really a little village in itself. Behind the master's house are workshops, storerooms, and the cabins where the Negroes live. In one house, meat is smoked and cured. In another house, cheese and butter are made. Then there are houses where the women spin and sew. There is a blacksmith shop, a carriage house, barns, and henhouses. There is even a big kitchen where the food is cooked before it is taken into the house to be served to the master and his family.

The slaves of a good master have many happy times after their hard day's work is done. Sometimes they gather around big bonfires and sing and dance. The sweet summer air is filled with the strumming of banjos, the music of fiddles, and the gay tones of mouth organs. The planter and his family often sit on the veranda of the big house and listen to the soft voices of the Negroes singing the beautiful songs of the old plantation.

Inside the master's house are carved walnut walls and highly waxed floors. The wide stairway leading to the second floor is polished until it shines like glass. The drawing room is large and has a white marble fireplace at one end. The mahogany chairs have red leather seats.

In the dining room, candlelight shines on fine silver, china, and glassware. There are beautiful mirrors and costly vases in the room. The wealthy plantation owners bring over the finest things they can buy in England. Their homes are both beautiful and comfortable.

The children of the wealthy planters do not go to school. They are taught by a *tutor*, or teacher, who lives on the plantation. The middle-class people sometimes send their boys to a little school taught by a minister, but the poor people can neither read nor write.

Most of the white people in the south are well to do and own large plantations. But there are also small homes and small farms. The people on the small farms do not have slaves. They do all their own work.

The planter and his family go to the Established Church of England. They often have to ride long distances to church. The mother and the smaller children ride in a carriage drawn by four prancing horses. A faithful servant dressed in a gay uniform drives the carriage. The father and the older boys ride horseback.

The southern colonists were gayer than the other colonists. Most of them had servants to help in the fields and about the house. They also had fewer church duties. They enjoyed dancing, horse racing, and hunting. They liked to play cards and to visit with their friends. They lived a busy and a happy life.

LIFE IN THE MIDDLE COLONIES

There were three groups of colonies: the New England Colonies, the Southern Colonies, and the Middle Colonies. The Middle Colonies were the colonies that had been settled by the Dutch and the Quakers. Even after the Dutch colonies were taken over by the English, many of the people kept their Dutch ways of living.

Their houses were tall and narrow and were built with the narrow end facing the street. Colored bricks were built into the walls in little patterns and every house had a small porch at the front door. At either side of the door was a bench where the people sat and visited with their neighbors.

The front door of the house was like two doors, one above the other. The housewife often opened the top half of the door so she could look out and wave to her friends.

165

On the first floor of the house were two rooms, a living room and a dining room. On the upper floor were the bedrooms. The kitchen was in a building back of the house. The family spent a great deal of time in the big kitchen. It was a gay, cheerful room. The furniture was painted in bright colors and on a railing around the walls stood shining pewter and beautiful china from Holland.

Near the great fireplace were all sorts of pots and pans. The thrifty Dutch housewives loved to cook, bake, sew, and clean. Their floors were always freshly scrubbed and sprinkled with white sand. Sometimes the sand was swept into pretty little patterns with a stiff broom.

The bedrooms upstairs were very cold in the wintertime. The tall four-poster beds had curtains all the way around to keep out the cold air. The people slept between two feather beds made of the finest goose down. The children's beds were so low they could be pushed underneath the big four-poster beds. They were called *trundle beds*.

166

The people wore plain, dark-colored clothes. The men and boys wore wide trousers, tight coats, and broad-brimmed hats. The women and girls wore full, swishing skirts, one on top of the other. On their heads they wore stiff white bands or stiffly starched caps.

In the wintertime the men, women, and children skated and went sleighing. The men and women even went to market on their skates. As they skated along the streets, they often carried their market baskets perched on top of their heads. At other times they hung the baskets on wooden yokes that rested on their shoulders.

Market day was always a happy occasion. Once a week the people gathered at the market place. A housewife who had more eggs, butter, or cheese than she needed brought them to market to sell. Then she bought the things she needed from the other women. Even the children loved market day, with its visiting, laughter, and fun for all.

Early each morning the housewives in some of the Dutch towns were awakened by the sound of bells. A man walked down the cobblestone streets with a wooden yoke on his shoulders. On each end of the yoke was a pail of milk. The bells on the yoke jingled merrily as he walked. When a housewife heard the bells, she ran out of doors with a pitcher in her hand. The man filled the pitcher with fresh milk from his pails and took the money she paid him.

Water was also sold to the Dutch housewives. The water cart came around every day. The women brought their buckets to be filled with the sparkling well water.

The Dutch people were very religious. They built many churches. They, like the Puritans, believed that everyone should learn to read the Bible. Schools were built almost as soon as the churches. The people in the Middle Colonies were religious, prosperous, and happy.

The Quakers also lived in the Middle Colonies. These honest, hard-working people lived very simple but busy lives. They wore plain brown or dark gray clothing. Their houses were comfortable, but not so gay as the homes of the Dutch. The Quakers had a saying, "Love thy neighbor as thyself." They tried to live as they believed.

They took care of the sick and the poor. They established hospitals. They built schools where a child might learn to do useful work. They tried to think not only of themselves, but also of their friends and neighbors.

EARNING A LIVING IN THE COLONIES

In the New England Colonies, the winters were very cold. Much of the soil was rocky. The people worked hard to make a living from the land.

Along the coast were little fishing and lumbering villages. Where the land was level, farming was carried on. Near streams of water, some of the people built mills and worked at manufacturing. But they all found it difficult to earn a living for their families.

The New England sea captains were much more fortunate. They carried on a good trade with the people of the West Indies. They took New England grain, lumber, cloth, and hides to the Indies. They traded these goods for West Indian sugar, fruit, and molasses. The sea captains even sailed as far as Africa and brought back slaves to sell to the Southern planters.

In the Southern Colonies the country was level, the climate warm. On the great plantations of the South, tobacco, rice, indigo, and cotton were raised. In some places there were also fishing and lumbering industries.

In the Middle Colonies the people lived on comfortable farms and carried on a good trade with the Indians. From these colonies shiploads of grain and furs were sent to England. The farmers raised grains, fruits, vegetables, and livestock. Some of the other men worked at lumbering, iron mining, and brickmaking.

Life in the Colonies Changes. The first settlers built very crude houses. They lived simply and worked hard. But as the years went by the little settlements became towns and cities. The people built better homes. They began to ship goods from one colony to another. They brought goods over from England. Life in the colonies became more and more as it had been in the Old World.

The homes of the later colonists were pleasant places in which to live. The homemade furniture had been replaced by beautiful furniture from England. The straw mattresses had been replaced by soft feather beds. The wooden dishes and trenchers were gone. The people now had pewter plates, china dishes, and fine silverware. They had beautiful linens and glassware. The colonies were growing and prospering!

Making a living was not easy, but the colonists worked hard. In the North, some of the men made their living at lumbering.

The northern colonists sent lumber, pitch, and tar to England. They built ships and sailed to nearly every port in the world.

Fishing was also a very important industry in the North. Many men made their living fishing off the coast of New England.

170

In the South,
the planters
shipped indigo,
rice, tobacco,
and cotton to
England, the
other colonies,
and to other
countries.

The Middle
Colonies sold
food grown on
their farms to
England, the
West Indies, the
other colonies,
and to the In-
dians.

The Middle
Colonies also
had other in-
dustries. Many
men worked at
lumbering, iron
mining, smelt-
ing, and brick-
making.

THINGS TO DO

1. Make a list of the things you have today that the early colonists did not have.

2. Make a diorama of a colonial kitchen. Show the different kinds of work that were done there and the tools that were used by the early colonists.

3. Draw pictures of a southern plantation. Make your pictures tell the story of life on the plantations.

4. In other books read stories about life in colonial days. Make a report to the class.

5. Find out how woolen and linen cloth are made today. Compare our modern ways with the way the colonists made their cloth.

6. Choose three of the words or phrases listed below. Write a short paragraph about each one. Make your paragraphs interesting. Read them to the class.

the common house	stocks	trencher
hickory wigwams	Pilgrim clothes	dugout houses
stockade	log cabins	bayberry candles
soapmaking	Betty lamps	wool cards
dame schools	flax brake	hornbook
New England Primer	whispering stick	foot stoves
plantation	warming pan	pillory
ducking stool	house-raising	spinning wheel

LET'S TALK ABOUT—

1. Why it was more difficult for the Pilgrims to build homes in the New World than it was for the later colonists.

172

2. Ways of living in the different colonies.

3. How life in the colonies was different from life today.

4. How the colonists helped us to have many of the things that we have today.

NEW WORDS

On a piece of paper write the words listed below. In front of each word write the number of the phrase that explains, or defines, the word. Put the words you did not know in your word file.

desire   repeal   determined   ammunition

musket   independent   survey   peaceably

1. to measure land

2. to wish for

3. in a peaceful manner

4. free and separate from

5. very firm

6. to cancel

7. a gun used in colonial times

8. bullets and powder used in guns

NAMES YOU WILL MEET IN THE NEXT STORY

Appalachian Mountains

Lexington

Declaration of Independence

War for Independence

Potomac River

Continental Congress

Paul Revere

Constitution of the United States

District of Columbia

General Montcalm

Before You Read the Story—

The thirteen colonies had grown very rapidly. The people no longer lived in crude houses. Many of them had homes as fine and as comfortable as those in England. They had good food and good clothes.

Most of the people still loved England. They were happy to be part of the British Empire. But before long they were to have a quarrel with the mother country. The quarrel was so serious it led the colonists to declare their independence and form a new nation.

After you have read this story, talk about the reasons the colonists thought England was taking away their freedom. Talk about how the colonists' desire to make their own laws led them to form a new nation. Talk about the reasons men will fight to be free.

A NEW NATION—
THE UNITED STATES OF AMERICA

More and more Englishmen came to the American colonies. Soon there was not enough room for all. New land had to be found for farms and for homes. There was but one way to move—*to the west.* People from the colonies began to push their way across the Appalachian Mountains.

Then a quarrel arose. The French claimed the land because Frenchmen had explored the Mississippi Valley. To them the great forests meant furs and money. To the English, the forests meant land for homes and for farms.

The French had settled a few towns in Canada and Louisiana. But most of the land they had explored was unsettled. The fur traders had built forts and trading posts throughout the Mississippi Valley, but they had not built homes. They wanted to get rich by trading with the Indians and then go back to France.

When the English began to move into the territory, the traders were very angry. "We will not give up the rich fur industry," they said. "The Indians will help us fight the British."

The French traders had trapped and hunted in the forests for some time. They had made friends with most of the Indians. Because of this friendship, they thought they could drive the British out of the territory. "The English are coming to take away your lands," they told the Indians. "We will help you fight to save them."

The Indians were quick to accept the idea. For nearly seventy-five years there was bitter fighting on the frontiers. During this time there were four separate wars. These wars are called the French and Indian Wars.

THE QUARREL IS SETTLED

After each war there was a time of peace. During peace-time, the English settlers worked hard. They built new homes and planted new crops. They built forts to protect their homes and their lands. They trained men to fight as the Indians fought. Finally the King sent over some soldiers from England. With the British soldiers to help them, the colonists decided it was time to settle the quarrel with the French.

The governor of Virginia sent George Washington to one of the French forts in the Ohio Valley. Washington asked the Frenchmen to leave the country, but they refused. Before long the last French and Indian War had begun!

A number of hard battles were fought, but the English armies were stronger than the French. Little by little, they pushed the French soldiers back to Quebec. At Quebec the French had a fort on a rock high above the St. Lawrence River. Here the Frenchmen made their last stand.

The French were commanded by General Montcalm, the English by General Wolfe. General Wolfe knew he must take the French fort if he were to win the war. But how could his soldiers climb the steep river-bank? How could they climb the jagged rock to the fort? All summer he searched for a way to

take the fort. At last he saw a tiny path leading up the side of the rock.

One dark night his soldiers crept silently up the path. When morning came, forty-five hundred English soldiers were lined up before the wall of Quebec. The surprised Frenchmen prepared for battle.

The fighting lasted for seven long hours. General Wolfe was killed leading his men. General Montcalm was wounded, and died a few hours later. Finally the French gave up. Quebec became an English city.

With the fall of Quebec, France lost most of her empire in America. She gave England all the land east of the Mississippi, except New Orleans. New Orleans and the land west of the Mississippi were given to Spain.

More and more people came to the colonies. Soon they became crowded. Men began to move to the west in search of new lands.

But the French did not like to have settlers moving into their territory. They asked the Indians to help them fight the British.

Four French and Indian Wars followed. England sent soldiers to help. The French were pushed back to Quebec.

The French fort was on a steep cliff high above the St. Lawrence. But the British found a tiny path leading up the rock.

One night the British crept silently up the path. They attacked the fort in the morning. After that battle, the French gave up.

The treaty of peace gave England territory that had been claimed by both France and Spain. France lost her empire in America.

1763
England wins lands that had been claimed by France and Spain

The wars with France had cost England a great deal of money. It would cost still more to keep soldiers in America to protect the colonists from the Indians. The Englishmen who made the laws believed the colonists should help to pay for the wars.

They passed a law called the *Stamp Act*. The Stamp Act said that the colonists had to put a stamp on all their business papers. The money received from the sale of the stamps was to be sent to England.

When the colonists heard they were to pay the stamp tax, they became very angry. In many of the colonies the people had helped to make their own laws. They did not like the idea of paying a tax for which they had not voted. "We will not buy the stamps," they said.

But the stamps were sent over. The colonists refused to buy them! Agents were sent over to sell the stamps. The colonists still refused! Benjamin Franklin told the English that the colonists would *never* buy the stamps.

Finally the Stamp Act was repealed. But soon a new law was passed. This law put a tax on such articles as tea, glass, lead, oil, and paper. Once again the colonists were angry. *"We will not pay a tax we did not vote for,"* they

said. "We will not buy any of the English goods. We will make our own or go without."

By this time England was determined the colonists should obey the new law. The colonists were determined they would not! Because of this, British soldiers in America had many quarrels with the colonists. After one quarrel, several men of Boston lay dead in the snow. The trouble between the mother country and the colonies was becoming serious!

The English merchants became worried. They were losing money because they could not sell to the colonists. The English government wanted to repeal the law, but King George III was stubborn. "We must show the colonists they *have* to obey the laws of England," he said. But finally the tax on everything except tea was repealed.

The colonists liked tea. But they decided they would not pay the tax. English ships loaded with tea sailed to the colonies. Philadelphia and New York sent the ships back to England. The people of Charlestown stored the tea in damp cellars and let it rot. In Boston the angry men took care of it in a different way.

THE BOSTON TEA PARTY

For days the tea ships lay anchored in Boston Harbor. The people would not allow the tea to be unloaded. But the ships could not return to England without a pass from the governor. What would happen?

One afternoon the captain of one ship went to ask the governor for a pass. The people decided it was time to act! When it was nearly dark, men dressed as Indians dashed down the street. With painted faces and waving tomahawks, they looked more like Indians than colonists. Straight toward the harbor they ran, shouting loudly.

When they reached the harbor, they climbed into rowboats that lay tied near the water's edge. With long, swift strokes they pushed the boats forward. Soon they had reached the big tea ships. Quickly they climbed on board. With sharp hatchets they broke open the chests of tea and dumped them overboard. In a few minutes, over three hundred chests of tea were sinking slowly into the waters of Boston Harbor!

181

When the King heard about the "Boston Tea Party" he was very angry. He declared that Boston should be punished and punished severely. He closed the Port of Boston to ships from the outside world.

Boston could no longer trade with any country nor with any colony. Food became scarce. Some of the people went hungry. When the other colonies heard how the King was punishing Boston, they quickly sent help. Wagons loaded with corn, fish, wheat, and other supplies arrived in Boston. Even the southern colonists sent loads of rice.

THE COLONISTS THINK OF INDEPENDENCE

The colonists were worried. Did the quarrel with England mean war? A call went out for a meeting to discuss the problem. On September 5, 1774, a group of men from all the colonies except Georgia met in Philadelphia. This group was called the First Continental Congress.

The Congress discussed the problem for many days. Some of the men wanted to settle the trouble peaceably. Others believed Americans should stand by their rights. Congress finally sent a letter to the King. The letter declared that the people had the right to govern themselves.

In Massachusetts the colonists began to gather guns, cannon, powder, and cannon balls. They stored them at Concord, about twenty miles from Boston. Farmers, shopkeepers, and tradesmen promised to fight at a moment's notice. For this reason they were called *minutemen*.

General Gage commanded the British soldiers at Boston. When he heard that the Americans were storing guns and ammunition at Concord, he made plans to seize the stores. An American leader named Dr. Joseph Warren heard of the British plans. *How could he warn the colonists?*

182

The road that ran from Boston into the country was guarded by the King's soldiers. But Dr. Warren worked out a scheme. Two men with fast horses were to wait just beyond the British guards. They were to watch in the direction of the Old North Church in Boston. If the British redcoats began to march, Dr. Warren was to flash a signal from the church steeple.

The men took their places along the road. Eagerly they waited. Minutes passed, and then hours. The horses pawed nervously at the ground. The men, too, became restless. Suddenly there was a flash of light. The signal from Dr. Warren! The British soldiers were marching to seize the supplies at Concord!

The two horsemen, Paul Revere and William Dawes, sprang to their horses. Swiftly through the black of night they rode. "The British are coming!" they called loudly as they rode through the countryside warning the settlers.

The minutemen heard the cry. They dressed hurriedly. Seizing their loaded muskets, they went out into the night. Quickly and quietly they joined their friends and neighbors. When dawn came, the British soldiers arrived at Lexington, a town just a few miles from Concord. They found their path barred by more than sixty armed colonists.

The soldiers and the minutemen fought at Lexington, at Concord, and on the way back to Boston. Men on both sides were killed. War between the colonies and the mother country now seemed certain.

When the English tried to enforce the Stamp Act, Franklin told them the colonists would not pay taxes they had not voted.

Many colonists made their own clothes, shoes, and other articles to avoid paying the tax on trade. Many bought smuggled goods.

Then England lifted the tax on everything but tea. The colonists in Charlestown stored the tea in damp cellars and let it rot.

In Boston, men dressed as Indians boarded tea ships and dumped the tea into the sea. *They would not pay a tax they had not voted!*

The Port of Boston was closed by the King. The angry colonists began to store guns, powder, and supplies at Concord.

British soldiers marched to seize the stores at Concord. Colonial minutemen met them. Shots rang out! War had begun!

Even after the battle of Lexington, the colonists tried to make peace with England. They tried again and again to get the King to allow them to help make their own laws. But the King always refused. Then England hired German soldiers to fight against the colonists.

When the colonists heard this, they knew there could be no peace. They must plan for war. On June 7, 1776, Richard Henry Lee from Virginia rose before the Congress. He proposed that the colonies should separate from England—that they should be free and independent. The Congress asked Thomas Jefferson to write a paper telling England that the colonies were going to be a free nation. The paper Jefferson wrote is called the *Declaration of Independence*. Congress accepted it on July 4, 1776. *For this reason July 4 is celebrated as the birthday of our nation.*

A few days later the people of Philadelphia gathered at their State House, or capitol. The Declaration of Independence was read to them. Then a large bell in the tower of the State House rang out. It told the world that the colonies declared themselves free and independent.

The people of Philadelphia wanted to show how important the Declaration was. They changed the name of their State House to *Independence Hall*. They changed the name of State House Yard to *Independence Square*. The bell that tolled the good news became the *Liberty Bell*.

A NEW FLAG IS CHOSEN

Even before the Declaration of Independence had been signed, George Washington was made commander of the colonial armies. Men from all of the colonies joined to help

186

win the fight for freedom. But the men had no flag to follow when they marched. They had no flag to fly proudly over their little camps.

When Washington met the soldiers near Boston, he had a flag with seven red stripes and six white stripes in it. The thirteen stripes stood for the thirteen original colonies. But in the corner of the flag was a symbol like the one used in the flag of England.

The colonies had declared themselves a new nation. The soldiers wanted a *new* flag! It is said that Betsy Ross and some of the other women helped Washington plan the first real American flag. It was like our flag today except for the field of blue. On the field of blue were thirteen stars that formed a circle.

Congress adopted the new flag June 14, 1777. Later it decided that "whenever a state comes into the union one star shall be added to the field of blue." *Because the flag was adopted on June 14, this date is Flag Day.*

THE AMERICAN FIGHT FOR FREEDOM

The American fight for freedom is called the War for Independence. When the war began, there was sharp and bitter fighting in all parts of the land. The ragged colonial armies fought bravely. But the soldiers of Great Britain were better trained, better armed, and better fed. At times it seemed as if the colonists could never win.

187

Perhaps the darkest hour of the war was the winter at Valley Forge. It was bitter cold that year. Snow and ice lay heavy on the ground. A few miles from the city of Philadelphia was Washington's army. The men were camped in crude huts. Each hut had a log fireplace, coated inside with mud. To keep the fires burning, the soldiers cut wood in the forest and dragged it to camp. As they worked, icy winds stung their hands and faces. Snow and sleet chilled their thin, shivering bodies.

For months the men had marched in the lines of battle. They were tired and hungry and cold. Their uniforms were ragged. Many of them had no shoes. Their frost-bitten, bleeding feet were wrapped in old rags and sacks.

Congress could not raise enough money to buy food, clothes, or medicine. The men lay on piles of straw. Many were sick and dying. It was a sad winter for George Washington. He went among the suffering men trying to cheer them. He used his own money to buy food and medicine.

Men who were not so brave would have given up! Some of the men did leave the army, but the others fought on. Then the people of France decided to help the colonists. With the help of the French soldiers, Washington forced the British to surrender. After nearly six and one half years of fighting, the colonies were free. A new flag waved over a new nation—*the United States of America.*

188

A NEW GOVERNMENT FOR A NEW NATION

After the War for Independence, the people felt they could return to their homes and live in peace. But there were still many problems. Congress did not really have the power to govern the people. It could pass laws, but it did not have the power to see that laws were obeyed.

Before long, the states began to quarrel among themselves. Wise leaders like George Washington knew that the nation would fail if the states could not agree. They realized that there must be a new and a stronger government. Fifty-five leaders from the different states traveled to Philadelphia. They met in Independence Hall where the Declaration of Independence was signed. The meeting they held is called the *Constitutional Convention.*

The Convention met to plan a new form of government. Washington was chairman of the meeting. He and wise old Benjamin Franklin helped to guide the men as they worked.

For many days the men worked hard to write our plan of government. The plan they wrote is called the *Constitution of the United States.* It has helped our country progress faster than any other nation in the world.

After the Constitution was adopted by the states, the people chose George Washington to lead the new nation. On April 30, 1789, Washington became the first president of the United States.

A GREAT AMERICAN

George Washington was a good leader and a great American. He did as much or more than any other man to help make the thirteen colonies free and independent. For this reason he is called *the father of his country.*

189

George Washington was born in Virginia on February 22, 1732. As a boy he had plenty of hard work, a little fun, and often the thrill of adventure. His plantation home lay near the western frontier. The hills near the frontier were covered with great forests. George and his friends did not go far into the forests, but they had many good times playing among the big trees.

When Washington was eleven years old his father died. His older half brother was away from home, and George became the head of the family. Not far from his plantation home was a school kept by a minister. Young George went to the school. He was very good in reading, writing, and arithmetic, but he found spelling difficult.

As he grew older, Washington learned to ride horses and to play outdoor games. This training helped him to become a good soldier. When he was sixteen, a rich man came to him. "I have bought a large tract of the Great Woods," he told Washington. "Will you go into the forest and survey, or measure, my land? I will pay you well." Washington took a companion and went to survey the land.

On this job and on other trips he learned to face hardships and danger. His fighting in the French and Indian Wars also taught him many things that helped him when he became commander in chief of the American army.

When Washington's half brother died, George inherited a plantation on the Potomac River. It was called Mount Vernon. Washington loved Mount Vernon. He liked to ride through the fields and watch the men at work. But when his country called him to lead the colonial armies, he left his plantation willingly.

Throughout the war he served his country without pay. He even bought food and clothing for the soldiers. During the bitter winter at Valley Forge, he must have longed for the comforts of his home at Mount Vernon. He must have wanted to go back to the plantation and forget the suffering he had seen. But he visited the plantation just once during the war, and then only for a few hours.

When the war was won, Washington wanted to stay home and rest. He did not want to be president. But the people would have no one else! A little sadly, but very proudly, he left his home at Mount Vernon to take up his duties as president.

Washington was a good president. He helped the young nation to become stronger and more firmly united. He helped the government win the respect of the people and the respect of other countries. When he was made president, New York City was the capital of our country. Then it was agreed that Philadelphia should be the capital for ten years. After that, a permanent capital was to be built on a piece of ground selected by Washington.

The site Washington chose was not far from his home at Mount Vernon, but on the other side of the Potomac River. The site of ground was named the *District of Columbia*. Our national capital and the home of our federal government are still in the District of Columbia.

George Washington served as president of our country for eight years. He served faithfully and well. The people wanted him to serve another term but he refused. "In a democracy no man should be president more than eight years," he said firmly. "The power of government must not remain in the hands of one man too long. If it does, the government will not serve the needs of the people."

After his "Farewell Address" to the people, Washington went back to his peaceful plantation at Mount Vernon. Two years later he died. The country had lost a great leader, a wise man, and a good friend!

When the colonists signed the Declaration of Independence, they declared that they were free and independent from England.

The colonists who were fighting for freedom wanted a new flag. The new flag had thirteen stars, one for each of the colonies.

The ragged colonial armies were often hungry and cold. Washington did everything he could to cheer the men at Valley Forge.

The courage of the colonial soldiers won them victory. The British surrendered to Washington. At last the colonies were free.

Delegates from the new states met to write a plan of government. The plan they wrote is the Constitution of the United States.

The states adopted the Constitution. Washington was chosen as our first president. He was a wise and able leader.

THINGS TO DO

1. Explain why the French and Indian Wars were a part of the story of our country.

2. Read stories or poems about Paul Revere, Nathan Hale, Benjamin Franklin, and John Paul Jones. Read them aloud to the class, or tell the class the most interesting things you read.

3. Make a series of pictures for your classroom showing how the colonies became the United States of America.

4. Write a short paragraph telling why we celebrate July 4 as our nation's birthday. Write another paragraph telling why we celebrate June 14.

5. Find a copy of the Declaration of Independence and a copy of the Constitution of the United States. You will not be able to read and understand all parts of these great documents, but you will enjoy seeing them.

LET'S TALK ABOUT—

1. Why the colonists refused to obey the tax laws passed by the English government.

2. Why the American soldiers who fought at Lexington were called minutemen.

3. Why the colonists thought the English government was taking away their freedom.

4. Why the ragged colonial armies fought better than the armies of Great Britain.

5. The reasons you think men will fight for freedom.

6. Reasons why the Constitution of the United States is a good plan of government.

NEW WORDS

The following words are used in the next story. You may not know all of them. Look up the meanings of the words you do not know. Then write sentences using each word. Put the words you did not know in your word file.

protection	huddled	puncheon
moccasins	language	linsey-woolsey
notched	information	community
pelt	sand bar	machinery
	current	

NAMES YOU WILL MEET IN THE NEXT STORY

Daniel Boone	New Orleans	Columbia River
Boonesboro	Sacajawea	Thomas Jefferson
Missouri River	Meriwether Lewis	

Englishmen establish Jamestown in 1607.

Hooker's congregation founds Connecticut.

The Pilgrims sign the Mayflower Compact.

New Amsterdam becomes New York.

Puritans build homes in the New World.

Maryland leaders buy land from Indians.

Roger Williams flees; founds Rhode Island.

William Penn establishes Pennsylvania.

North and South Carolina are settled.

Colonists protest the English tax on tea.

Delaware and New Jersey become colonies.

The fight for independence begins.

Oglethorpe sends settlers to Georgia.

The Declaration of Independence is signed.

Colonists move west to build new homes.

Washington becomes our first president.

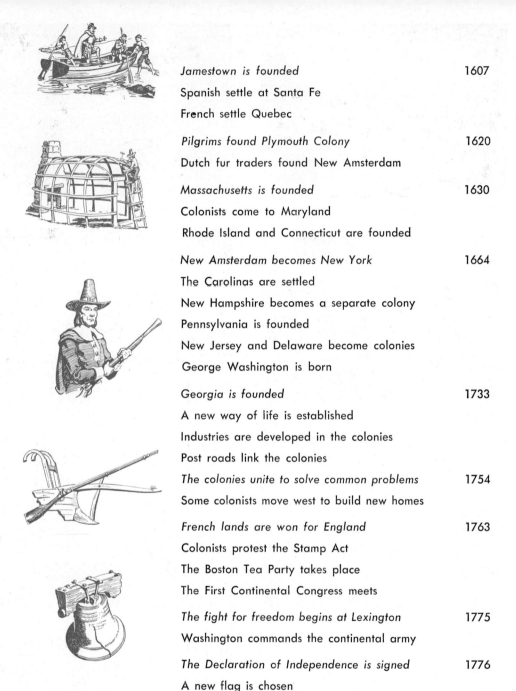

Jamestown is founded   1607

Spanish settle at Santa Fe

French settle Quebec

Pilgrims found Plymouth Colony   1620

Dutch fur traders found New Amsterdam

Massachusetts is founded   1630

Colonists come to Maryland

Rhode Island and Connecticut are founded

New Amsterdam becomes New York   1664

The Carolinas are settled

New Hampshire becomes a separate colony

Pennsylvania is founded

New Jersey and Delaware become colonies

George Washington is born

Georgia is founded   1733

A new way of life is established

Industries are developed in the colonies

Post roads link the colonies

The colonies unite to solve common problems   1754

Some colonists move west to build new homes

French lands are won for England   1763

Colonists protest the Stamp Act

The Boston Tea Party takes place

The First Continental Congress meets

The fight for freedom begins at Lexington   1775

Washington commands the continental army

The Declaration of Independence is signed   1776

A new flag is chosen

The fight for freedom is won   1781

The United States Constitution is written

George Washington becomes our first president   1789

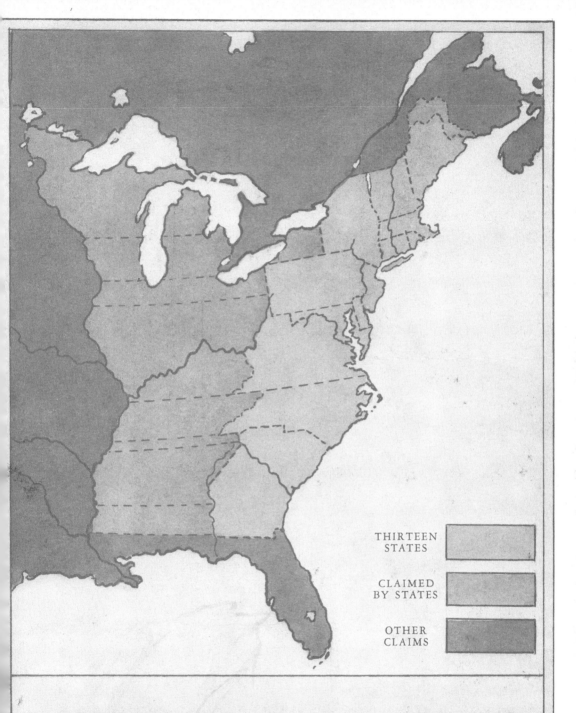

THIRTEEN
STATES

CLAIMED
BY STATES

OTHER
CLAIMS

After the War for Independence, the thirteen colonies along the Atlantic seacoast became the United States of America. The states also claimed the land to the west because many Americans had built homes in the territory.

Part III—THE NATION MOVES WESTWARD

The frontiers of our country were pushed farther and farther west. Each year hundreds of families packed their belongings and followed the trails to the west.

The *frontier* is the newest edge of settled country. It is the land on the edge of the wilderness. The *pioneers* are the first people to settle in a new country. They help to prepare the way for the others who follow them.

Even before the War for Independence, the pioneers had started to move to the west. Many of their problems were the same as the problems faced by the colonists.

After you have read this story, tell how the lives of the pioneers and the colonists were alike. Talk about how the borders of our country were moved farther west.

THE PIONEERS
MOVE TO THE WEST

After the War for Independence was won, our country reached west to the Mississippi and north to Canada. Indians lived in the great forests, but they did not make use of the fertile lands. The rich territory was waiting, almost untouched, for the white men to settle there.

PREPARING THE WAY FOR THE WESTERN SETTLER

The government divided the western country into large squares and the squares into smaller pieces of land. Each piece of land was given a number to help the settler in choosing the ground he wanted. Then the land was priced so low that most men could afford to buy it.

The government also made laws to help the westward moving settlers. Each town was to elect its own officers and make its own laws. Schools and churches were to be built. When there were enough people in a territory, it was to become a state. The new state was to have the same rights and powers as the old states.

Stories of the rich lands to the west spread quickly. Men began to dream of plowing and planting fields where great forests stood. They began to dream of building towns and cities. But they did more than dream! They began to make their dreams come true. Families began to pack their household goods, a few tools, a gun, some

203

powder, a spinning wheel, a few clothes, and perhaps a bed. Slowly but surely they began to move toward the west.

DANIEL BOONE—A GREAT PATHFINDER

Not all men traveled to the west in search of homes. Some went because they liked to explore new country. They loved to push farther and farther into the wilderness. These men were called *pathfinders*. They opened up new paths for the settlers to follow.

Even before the colonies became free, the pathfinders were moving to the west. As they traveled, they made blazes, or cuts, on the trunks of trees. The blazes left white spots that could be seen for long distances. The later travelers often followed the marked trees as they journeyed through the dense woods.

Perhaps the most famous of the pathfinders was Daniel Boone. Boone lived on the frontier in North Carolina. In his coonskin cap, his leather moccasins, and his deerskin shirt and trousers, he loved to go hunting in the forest. His eyes were sharp; his aim straight and true. It was not often a deer or a bear escaped him. Once when he killed a bear in the forest he carved on a tree, "D. Boon cilled a Bar on this tree in 1760."

Over and beyond the mountains near Boone's home were the hills of Kentucky. In Kentucky there were rich meadows of bluegrass, black soil, and good hunting. There were also savage Indians ready to kill any white settler who tried to make a home there.

But Boone knew no fear! One day he and some companions began the long journey to Kentucky. For days they climbed steep hills, waded or swam swift streams, and crept through the forests.

204

At last they came to the country Boone had dreamed about. Never before had he seen so many wild animals. Never before had he seen such tall grass and such good soil. But the Indians did not like the white men's coming into their territory. They killed one of Boone's companions and frightened the others away.

By this time Boone's brother had joined him. The two men hunted and trapped in the forest. Several times Boone's brother went home for supplies, but Boone always stayed on alone. He did not even have a dog for a companion. But he was happy. He roamed through the forests, hunting and exploring the country. "What a wonderful place to build a settlement," he often thought.

After two years he returned to North Carolina. He wanted to take his family and some of his friends back to Kentucky. He helped to build a road over what had been only an old Indian path. The road was called the *Wilderness Road.*

Boone led his party over the Wilderness Road into Kentucky. There they built the town of Boonesboro. To protect themselves from the Indians, they built their log cabins into the walls of a high fort. At each corner of the fort they built a strong blockhouse. The only entrance to the fort was a heavy gate. With this protection, the settlers could defend themselves for many hours.

Other forts were soon built near the one at Boonesboro. The settlers lived inside the forts and raised crops in the rich soil outside. Life was not easy for these early pioneers. Often they heard the cry, "Indians are in the woods!" When the cry came, the people hurried inside the fort. They closed the big gates and fastened them tight. The women and children huddled together in the safest corner of the cabin. The men pushed their rifles through holes in the log walls and stood ready to defend their homes.

As the Indians crept forward, the crack of the settlers' guns rang out sharply. The Indians returned the fire with whooping war cries. Sometimes the fight continued for hours! The Indians tried to throw burning torches onto the cabins to set them on fire. The settlers had to watch for the torches and put them out.

It was not often the Indians could capture a fort. But sometimes the settlers were killed or wounded. It was always a relief when the red men stole back into the deep woods and the fight was over.

Daniel Boone was captured by the Indians several times, but he always escaped. Once he was made a member of an Indian tribe. The Indians pulled all the hair from his head except a thick bunch on top. They painted his body a rich brownish red. They painted a red and green and black design on his face. Then they dressed him in Indian clothes and he looked like a real Indian.

They watched him carefully as he moved about the Indian village. But Boone acted happy and contented. Then he heard that the Indians were going to attack Boonesboro. He could pretend no longer—he must find a way of escape.

He watched his chance. When it came, he crept quietly into the forest. Then he began to run. For three days and three nights he raced through the woods. When the Indians came to capture the fort, they found Boone there helping the men to defend it.

After some years the call of the frontier came once more to the great pathfinder. He traveled still farther to the west. He made new trails through the wilderness and helped to open up new paths for the pioneers. He loved life best when he was in wild, new country. "I have room to breathe there," he once said.

HELPING THE WESTERN FARMER

With the westward moving settlers came a new problem. The War for Independence had long been over. But the settlers found that the British still had forts between the Appalachian Mountains and the Mississippi River. Washington sent a man to England to try to settle the question. The two governments made a treaty, and the British soldiers were sent back to England. For the first time, the settlers felt free to build homes.

A treaty with Spain also helped the western farmers. To send their crops to the eastern markets, the farmers had to ship them down the Mississippi. Spain still owned New Orleans. She charged a high tax on all river shipping. A treaty between the United States and Spain opened the river for free shipping. The settlers could now make money from their new farms.

Thomas Jefferson was the third president of the United States. During his long and busy life he helped to make our country great. Often he has been called "the friend of the people." He liked the poor people and did all he could to help them. He wanted them to vote and to hold office. "In a free nation the rich people should not do all the ruling," he said wisely.

At one time he named the three things he wished to be remembered for. First, for writing the Declaration of Independence. Second, for writing a Virginia law that gave everyone the right to worship God as he pleased. Third, for beginning the University of Virginia.

When Jefferson became president, our country reached to the Mississippi. West of the Mississippi was the Louisiana Territory, which belonged to France. The Louisiana Territory stretched from the mouth of the Mississippi northwestward to the Rocky Mountains. Spain had owned part of the territory but she had given it to France. She had also given New Orleans to France.

The western settlers were worried again. They heard that France was going to close the river. If France closed the Mississippi to shipping, the settlers could not buy machinery from the east. They could not buy cloth, sugar, shoes, and many other things they needed. They could not ship their produce to the eastern markets.

France *did* close the river. President Jefferson sent men to France to try to buy New Orleans. At first the ruler of France refused to sell. Then he changed his mind. He offered the United States New Orleans and all of the Louisiana Territory for only fifteen million dollars.

The American delegates had not been told to buy Louisiana. But it seemed too good a chance to miss. After the papers were signed, our minister to France said, "We have lived long, but this is the noblest act of our lives!"

Eighteen years later, the United States purchased Florida from Spain. Our borders east of the Mississippi became as they are today!

ACROSS THE COUNTRY TO THE PACIFIC

The United States now owned Louisiana. But little was known about the new territory. What kind of plants and trees were growing there? What kind of animals roamed the hills and valleys? Were there valuable minerals in the Rocky Mountains? Were the Indians friends or enemies?

President Jefferson sent a party of men to explore the Louisiana Territory. He chose Captain Meriwether Lewis and Captain William Clark to head the party. On May 14, 1804, the little group set out from St. Louis, Missouri. With them they took beads, knives, hatchets, mirrors, and bright-colored cloth to give to the Indians along the way.

All summer the men paddled up the muddy Missouri River. Sometimes the current of the water was so strong they had to go on shore and tow the boats upstream. At other times they had to make rough carts and pull the boats on land until they could travel on the water again.

When winter came they were among the Mandan Indians in North Dakota. They decided to spend the winter there. One day a French trader came into camp. With him was his young wife, Sacajawea, often called the *Bird Woman*. The trader could speak English and several Indian languages.

As soon as Captain Lewis met him, he knew the old trader would be of great help to his little party. "Will you go with us?" he asked the Frenchman. When spring came, the trader and his Indian wife went with the explorers.

Sacajawea's real home had been far away beyond the mountains. As a little girl she had been brought to live near the Mandan Indians. There the trader had bought and married her. But the Bird Woman still remembered her old home. She was eager to go back.

The men traveled up the Missouri River until they reached the mountains. Then they left their boats and traveled on foot. Sacajawea carried her baby on her back and tramped along with the men.

Through the mountain wilderness they pushed their way. Then a strange thing happened. The Bird Woman had been over the trail only once before. But she began to see things and places she could remember. Before long she became the guide for the weary men.

Finally the little party crossed over the mountains. By this time their food was almost gone. The men were tired and discouraged. Lewis and Clark went ahead to find a friendly Indian tribe. Soon they sent for Sacajawea to come and tell them what the Indians said.

The Bird Woman came into the tent and sat down in a circle with the men. She began to talk the Indian language. Then suddenly she became quiet. She looked long and hard at the chief. In a moment she jumped up, ran toward him, and said, "Brother!" She told him her story and then he, too, remembered. "Welcome, little princess," he said. "You have returned to your own people."

Sacajawea told her brother how kind the white men had been to her and how much they needed help. The chief gave them food and ponies. He sent some of his braves to guide them through the mountain passes. Without his help the men could not have continued their journey!

Sacajawea rode one of the ponies as the men traveled westward. At last they came to a river. In boats given to them by the Indians, they set sail upon the river. They followed it until they came to the Snake River. They followed the Snake River until they came to the waters of a still larger river. They had reached the swift Columbia.

Day after day the men followed the Columbia River westward. Clouds of fog lay heavy on the river. Often the men had to drift blindly with the current of the water. Then came a happy day! November 7, 1805, was a day without fog. The men could see in the distance the waters of the blue Pacific. After months of weary travel, they had reached the end of their journey!

The men stayed on the Pacific Coast all winter. Then they began the journey homeward. They reached St. Louis in September, 1806. They had been gone over two years.

It was not an easy journey that the men had made! For months they had traveled among strange and sometimes unfriendly Indians. They had made trails over high and dangerous mountains. They had crossed streams and rivers where there were no bridges.

Through heavy snowstorms, ice, and freezing weather they had fought their way. They had gone hungry. They had even eaten dog and horse meat. But not once had they lost courage! Day after day they had struggled on until they had finally reached the Pacific.

The great journey made by Lewis and Clark gave the government much valuable information. After their return, the two men wrote reports of their journey. They described the country and the Indian tribes they visited. They told about the soil, the plants, and the animals.

Their reports made the people eager to make homes in the new country. Before many years, the wagons of the pioneers were traveling over trails made by the explorers.

A VISIT WITH A PIONEER FAMILY ALONG THE OHIO

The pioneers and the colonists lived much the same. They both built homes in a strange wilderness. They both cleared the forests and planted crops. They both made their own clothes and their own furniture. Some of the things they did were different, but they were each settling a new land. The task of each was difficult.

The first pioneers were the men and women who settled beyond the Appalachian Mountains. A story written by a boy from one of these pioneer families might have been much like this one.

The day came when we were to start the long journey to the West. My sister and I were so excited we could scarcely eat the breakfast that had been sent to us by a neighbor. The day before we had worked hard. The covered wagon that was to be our home for many days had been packed. It now stood beside the porch. The oxen had been harnessed to it and everything seemed ready.

Father called to mother. "Did you make a list of the things that are packed?" he asked.

Mother came out of the house. "Yes, John," she answered. "Shall I read it to you?" From the paper in her hand she read, "Iron kettles, spinning wheel, a plow, a barrel of salted meat, tools, guns, gunpowder, molasses, tea, some food, a bed, a chest of clothes, some seeds, and the family Bible."

Father nodded his head. "I think that will keep us going until we can harvest our first crop," he said thoughtfully.

It was now almost time to start. Our neighbors came over to

say good-by. Mother cried a little and then climbed into the covered wagon. She held the baby in her arms and put my little brother on the seat beside her. Then father started the oxen and our journey had begun.

Father walked beside the wagon. My sister and I drove the cow. When my sister got tired she rode in the wagon, too. I wondered if father would ever let me ride—he often said that boys should not get tired.

The days seemed long as we moved slowly toward the west. The roads were rough and sometimes muddy. When it rained we all slept in the wagon. On clear nights father and I slept on the ground. I did not like to sleep on the ground, but in the morning it was fun to eat breakfast around the campfire.

Finally we came to a town on the banks of the Ohio River. Father bought some lumber and built a flatboat. The flatboat looked like a great raft. In the center of the boat was a little cabin. Father said the family would sleep and live there while we made the journey down the river.

Before we left, father bought some pigs, ducks, and chickens. He put them on the flatboat in little pens. Then we put the wagon and our other things on the boat and we were ready to leave.

As the flatboat sailed down the Ohio River we had many exciting times. One day our boat ran into a sand bar. We had to take long poles and push and push until we were free and sailing downstream again. Another day the wind drove us to the bank of the river. We got caught in some buried logs for a while. Then we ran into low-hanging trees. The branches of the trees snapped and cracked as we tried to free ourselves.

We landed at a little town far down the river. Father took the boat apart to save the lumber and the nails. Both were scarce on the frontier. Then he found a place for mother and us children to stay while he went to look for a farm.

In a few weeks he came back. "I have found a piece of ground

213

with rich black soil," he said. "There is a spring nearby. It will be a good place to build our home."

We packed our belongings in the wagon and went to the place father had chosen. Mother was glad that other settlers lived nearby. It would make it easier for us to get started.

Father began to cut down the trees and to prepare the logs for building a house. Friendly neighbors came by and helped him. When enough logs were ready, the people from miles around came to help with the house-raising.

The men rolled the rough logs to the spot father had cleared for the house. Then they notched the logs so they would fit one on top of the other. With this done, they began to raise the walls of the house. In a short time they were through. Then they made a roof and covered it with bark. A door of logs and a log shutter for the window were made next.

Then father called to the children who had been standing around watching the men work. "Bring us wet clay from the river-bank," he said. "You may start to fill in the cracks between the logs while we plaster the inside of the chimney."

It was fun filling the cracks with soft, wet clay. Mother came over and watched us. "When the clay dries, it will become very hard," she said. "It will keep the wind from blowing through the house. It will also keep the chimney from catching on fire."

Then she looked inside the cabin. "We will have to be satisfied with a dirt floor for the present," she said. "But when father has time he will make a puncheon floor, or a floor of split logs. He will also make wooden shingles for the house."

While the men had been working, the women had been busy, too. A feast had been spread out under the tall trees. The neighbor women had made corncakes, dried-apple pies, fried chicken, roast pork, and many other good things to eat.

While the food was being eaten, there was much laughing and talking. Everyone tried to make us feel welcome. It was a good

214

feeling to know that our neighbors were so friendly. The frontier did not seem so strange and lonely!

That night we all slept on the dirt floor of the new house. The next day father began to make furniture for the little cabin. He made beds, a table, a bench, and some three-legged stools. Mother brought in the spinning wheel, the big iron kettles, and some of the other things we had brought with us. The cabin began to seem like a real home.

All during the summer we worked hard. The trees near the house were cut down and a garden was planted. The garden was tended carefully so there would be corn and pumpkins in the fall. Wild honey was gathered and stored.

Father made a puncheon floor for the cabin. He made wooden shingles for the roof. Mother put oiled paper over the little window. She threw bearskin rugs on the floor. Our cabin was as warm and comfortable as those of our neighbors!

The pioneer women did many of the things the colonial women had done. They dipped candles. They dried fruits and vegetables. They made cheese and butter. Their food was cooked in large kettles that hung over the fireplace. Soap was made over a fire in the back yard.

Wool was carded and flax was spun. A cloth woven from both wool and flax was used for most of their clothes. The cloth was called *linsey-woolsey*.

Other clothes were made from the skins of animals. When an animal was killed, the pelt was removed with a sharp knife. The pelt was salted or dried thoroughly to keep it from rotting. Then it was put into a large tub of lye and water, or it was soaked in wet wood ashes. This made the hair, or fur, loose so it could be scraped off easily.

Many of the pioneer boys and girls helped to scrape the hair from the animal skins. They worked very carefully so they would not tear or cut the skin. After the loose hair was scraped off, the skin was put in another tub filled with a liquid made from water and black-oak bark. The skin was left in this liquid for several months. Then it was taken out and carefully scraped again.

By now the skin was clean but it was stiff and hard. It could not be used for clothing. To make the skin soft, it was rubbed with bear's grease, lard, and tallow. The fat was first worked into the skin. Then the skin was rubbed and rubbed until it was soft and ready for use. Preparing animal skins in this way is called *tanning leather*.

The clothes of the pioneers were very plain. The women wore long, full skirts and tight waists that buttoned down the front. Little shawls were thrown over their shoulders, and on their heads they wore sunbonnets.

The men wore long trousers made of a heavy, dark material. The legs of the trousers were often stuffed into high-topped boots. Instead of ties the men wore bright-colored handkerchiefs around their necks. In warm weather they did not wear coats; they wore vests made of heavy cloth or leather.

The boys and girls were dressed much as their mothers and fathers were dressed. They looked quite "grown-up" when they were still children.

The pioneers worked hard, but they also had happy times. They held husking bees, logrollings, quilting bees, and house-raisings. They had spelling matches and community singing in their little log schools and churches. The people enjoyed these social gatherings. It was pleasant, after a hard day's work, to visit with friends and to enjoy the feasts of good food prepared by the women.

The boys and girls had merry times, too. In the winter they liked to go skating and sleighing. In summer they played many of the games that girls and boys play today.

The little girls made rag dolls and stuffed them with wool combings or pieces of old cotton. They made doll clothes from pieces of cloth they found in their mother's rag bag of worn-out clothing.

The boys made their own marbles. Thick wet clay was rolled between the hands until it was the shape of a marble. Then it was rolled in fine sand and baked in the fire until it was hard. Sometimes the marbles were a little out of shape, but the boys had fun playing with them.

The young people enjoyed dancing best of all. After a cornhusking bee the floor of the barn was cleared. Then the fiddlers took their places and the men chose partners. The couples formed sets for an old square dance. Fiddles were tuned up and the lively music began.

The voice of the caller was loud and hearty. "Cast Off," "Swing Your Partner," and "Right and Left" were familiar calls as the young people swung through set after set of the dance. Merry laughter mingled with the brisk music. The cares of the day were forgotten!

As time went on, more and more people moved to the West. They took their possessions along in big covered wagons.

Daniel Boone, and other pathfinders, blazed trails through the wilderness to guide the settlers as they journeyed to the West.

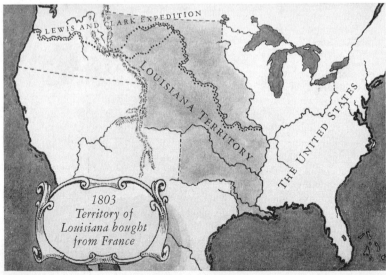

LEWIS AND CLARK EXPEDITION

LOUISIANA TERRITORY

THE UNITED STATES

1803
Territory of
Louisiana bought
from France

In 1803, the United States bought Louisiana from the French. This opened up a vast, new territory in the Northwest.

Two explorers named Lewis and Clark traveled over the new territory. Their reports helped the country and the pioneers.

Pioneers moving into the Ohio Valley traveled down the river on flatboats until they came to land they wanted to settle.

When the pioneers found a piece of land they wanted, they cleared forests, planted crops, and built homes for their families.

THINGS TO DO

1. Begin a booklet called "The Pioneers Who Settled the West." In your booklet, draw pictures of pioneer life. Write a short story about each picture. You will want to save your booklet to add other stories about the pioneers.

2. Make an outline map of the United States. Color the Louisiana Territory green.

3. On a large sheet of wrapping paper, make an outline map of the United States. Make your map a picture story of the journey of Lewis and Clark. Outline the trail the men followed to the Northwest. Talk about other things you might put on your map to tell the story of their journey. Would a picture of the Bird Woman belong on the map? Would you show the men traveling down the Columbia River in boats?

4. Read more about the life of Thomas Jefferson. Tell the class the most interesting things you read.

5. Learn a square dance or the Virginia Reel. You will enjoy dancing them as much as the pioneers did.

LET'S TALK ABOUT—

1. The difference between a pathfinder and a pioneer.

2. Why the first pioneers moved to the West.

3. Why the purchase of the Louisiana Territory was an important part of our country's story.

4. Why the journey made by Lewis and Clark was important to the westward moving people.

5. Why Portland, Oregon, has a statue of Sacajawea, the Bird Woman, in its city park.

6. Things that both the colonists and the pioneers did.

NEW WORDS

You will find the following words in the next story. Match the words and the phrases. Look up the meanings of the words you do not know. Put these words in your word file.

parched	a waterway built by man
caravan	a company of travelers
hymn	dried by great heat
summit	a religious song
sagebrush	the highest point
canal	a low gray-green bush that grows in the desert

NAMES YOU WILL MEET IN THE NEXT STORY

Alamo	Colonel Travis	Sam Houston
Stephen F. Austin	Mormons	Sacramento
Cherokees	Lone Star Republic	Marcus Whitman
Narcissa Whitman	Brigham Young	Gadsden Purchase

Before You Read the Story—

The story of how our country grew is like a map that unfolds. The map first unfolds to show the land along the Atlantic seacoast. Colonists are living there.

Then the map unfolds to the Mississippi River. People begin to settle and to build homes in the land between the Appalachian Mountains and the river.

When the land there is settled, the map unfolds again. People move to a new section of land still farther west. When that section is settled, other people move farther and farther west. Again the map unfolds.

As the years go by, our country grows larger and larger. The map unfolds again and again. In time our country reaches from the Atlantic to the Pacific. After you have read this story, talk about the new sections of country that were added to our map. Talk about why and how the pioneers built homes in the west.

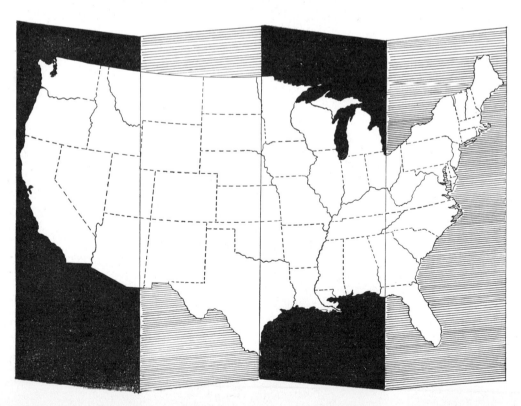

THE PIONEERS
PUSH FARTHER WEST

TEXAS WINS HER FREEDOM FROM MEXICO

Inside the walls of the *Alamo* the Texans heard the demand, "Lay down your arms and surrender." The call came from Santa Anna, commander of the Mexican army.

When the Texans heard the demand, a burst of cannon shot rang from the mission walls! Colonel Travis, commander of the Texans, said to his men, "We have answered the demand of Santa Anna with cannon shot. Our flag still waves from the mission walls."

There were more than one hundred eighty Texans inside the Alamo. The Mexican army was nearly twenty times as large. General Santa Anna said to his men, "We have given the Texans warning. In this battle there are to be no prisoners. Every man is to be killed!"

With great cries the Mexican soldiers clambered over the mission walls. Their swords flashed; their guns cracked. Little by little they fought their way forward.

Each Texan stood his ground, fighting until he fell dead. The shouting Mexicans pushed on—over the crumpled bodies. When the battle was over, the courtyard, the walls, and the mission floor ran red with blood. Not one Texan was left alive. Each man had fought to his death, defending his freedom and the honor of Texas.

Ever since that day, March 6, 1836, the battle cry of Texas soldiers everywhere has been "Remember the Alamo!"

General Sam Houston, a famous Texas hero, was born in Virginia, March 2, 1793. When he was a boy his father died and his family moved to Tennessee. On the rugged frontiers of Tennessee, he played with the Indian children and grew to love them and to respect their people.

After he was grown, he became a soldier and helped the United States win several battles. Then he married and later became governor of Tennessee. Unhappy in Tennessee, he left his office and went back to live with the Cherokee Indians. He thought he would enjoy an easy, carefree life.

But the call of the frontier was in his blood. He traveled to Texas and was there when Texas declared her independence from Mexico. A good soldier, he was chosen commander of all Texan forces.

When he heard of the plight of the men at the Alamo,

he planned to send help. Then he heard that the mission had fallen. Gathering his forces, he prepared to make a final stand against Santa Anna.

Santa Anna and his men were camped by the San Jacinto River. One afternoon some of them were sleeping, others were watering their horses. Silently, and without warning, General Houston and his soldiers appeared at the edge of the woods. They swept out into the open and rushed toward the Mexicans, shouting, "Remember the Alamo!"

The surprised Mexicans ran. The Texans ran after them. In a short time the Mexicans surrendered. When the terms of peace were signed, Texas became an independent nation.

Before this Texas had been a part of Mexico. After Texas became a separate nation, it was called The Republic of

Texas. Houston was chosen its first president.

Later, when Texas became a part of the United States, Houston was one of its first senators. The other senators liked him, but they thought him a strange man. He wore his hair long and when the weather was cold he wrapped himself in an Indian blanket.

Houston dreamed of doing many things for his beloved state. He was not able to do all that he dreamed, but he helped Texas in many ways.

 ANOTHER GREAT TEXAN

Stephen F. Austin has often been called the *father of Texas*. He and Sam Houston did much to make Texas the great state that it is today. For this reason two of the most important cities in Texas are named for them. Austin, the capital of Texas, is named for Stephen Austin. Houston, another important city, is named for Sam Houston.

When Austin first went to Texas, the territory was ruled by Mexico. Austin asked the Mexican government for permission to start a colony. After he received permission he took three hundred families there to settle.

Austin soon grew to love the rich new country. He wanted more and more people to come there. He went through the southern states telling the people about the wide prairies and the rich soil of Texas. "Any crop will grow there," he said proudly.

In a few years twenty-five thousand Americans were living in Texas. But there was often trouble between the rulers of Mexico and the settlers. Austin traveled to Mexico

City. He tried to have Texas made a separate state in the Mexican Republic. The Mexican government put him in prison and kept him there for many months.

When Austin finally returned home, he found that the Texas leaders were ready to break with Mexico. He, too, believed this was the best thing to do. In every way he could, he helped to win the fight for freedom.

When Houston became president of The Republic of Texas, he made Austin Secretary of State. Austin had served Texas long and well. He wanted to live quietly, but he died serving the country that he loved.

THE UNITED STATES GETS THE SOUTHWEST

Texas became a state in 1845. Not long after this, Texas and the Mexican government began to quarrel over a small section of country. The boundary line between the two had not been clearly marked. Texas and Mexico both claimed the same piece of ground. American citizens had also filed damage claims against Mexico.

President Polk sent United States soldiers into Texas. They had a small fight with some Mexican soldiers near the Rio Grande, and Congress declared war.

The United States won the war. The terms of peace gave our country the great Southwest. This included what is now California, New Mexico, Utah, Nevada, part of Colorado, and most of Arizona. The United States gave Mexico fifteen million dollars, and settled the claims of the Americans against the Mexican government.

Six years later the rest of Arizona was purchased from Mexico for ten million dollars. This is called the *Gadsden Purchase*. The Gadsden Purchase made our southern border as it is today.

Settlers were led to the rich lands of Texas by Stephen F. Austin. At that time Texas was still a part of the Republic of Mexico.

The people in Texas were not happy under Mexican rule. They declared themselves free and called their state the Lone Star Republic.

But the Texans had to fight for their right to freedom. At the Alamo they fought until every man was killed by the Mexicans.

Houston and his Texas armies forced Santa Anna to surrender. Texas won the right to become a free and independent state.

After Texas became a state in the Union, Mexico and the United States fought about the boundary between Texas and Mexico.

The war was soon over. The peace treaty gave us lands north of the Rio Grande. Later we made the Gadsden Purchase.

1845–1853
New lands added by annexation of Texas, a treaty with Mexico, and Gadsden Purchase.

DISPUTED

Ceded by Mexico
1848

THE UNITED STATES

Gadsden Purchase
1853

Texas
1845–8

MEXICO

The Indian chief and his three warriors had come from faraway Oregon. They had made the long journey to St. Louis to talk with the white men.

"Hunters and traders have come into our country," the Indians said. "They have told us about the white man's God. We want to know more. We want to know how to live so your God will be pleased with us. We want to have the Book of Heaven." *The Book of Heaven was the Bible.*

The church people were very interested. "We will send missionaries to the Oregon country," they decided. "We will teach the Indians about God. We will teach them how to improve their ways of living."

The country along the Pacific Coast *north of California* was called Oregon. At first England and the United States both claimed the land. Then it was decided that each country should have equal rights to settle and to trade there. When the missionaries began the long journey into Oregon, the land belonged to both countries.

Dr. Marcus Whitman was one of the first missionaries to go into Oregon. With him went his wife, Narcissa. Sacajawea had traveled over the mountains into Oregon. But Narcissa Whitman and a friend were the first white women to make the long and dangerous journey.

The Whitman party started from St. Louis in 1836. For weeks they traveled over the hot dusty plains. The women rode in the wagon. The men rode on horseback.

When they came to the Rocky Mountains the wagons had to be left behind. The mountain passes were too narrow—the roads too steep—for the big wagons. Dr. Whitman made a two-wheeled cart and loaded it with provisions. Then the little party went on.

230

The women now rode on horseback the same as the men. The trail led through mountain passes so narrow that the sun could not reach them. It wound round and round, over streams of water, and up steep hillsides.

Finally the Rocky Mountains were crossed. Traveling was not so difficult, but the party was weary. Miles and miles of desert sagebrush stretched ahead. Would the Oregon country never be reached?

At last the little group came to the Columbia River. The end of the journey was in sight! Dr. Whitman built a mission near where the town of Walla Walla, Washington, stands today. He and his wife soon made friends with the Indians. They taught the red men about God. They showed them how to till the soil, plant crops, and how to harvest the grains and vegetables.

Later, when settlers came into the Oregon country, the mission was a welcome stopping place. The Whitmans helped everyone they could. Mrs. Whitman took care of boys and girls whose parents had died along the trail. She gave many of the travelers food and clothes.

At one time there was a great sickness among the Indians.

Dr. Whitman had often cured them when they had been sick. But this time he could not help them. Some of the Indians were angry. "The white doctor is to blame," they said. Without warning they attacked the mission.

The mission was completely destroyed. Dr. Whitman and his wife lost their lives. But they had helped to open up the great Northwest.

Before long, stories of the rich soil and the mild climate in Oregon spread throughout the East. Thousands of families began to move to the new territory. On the way to the West, the people suffered many hardships. Heat, cold, hunger, thirst, danger, and death seemed to wait for them on the trail. But they went on and on!

When they came to the beautiful Oregon Valley they cleared the land, built homes, and planted crops. In a short while thousands of settlers had moved into Oregon.

But the land still belonged to both England and the United States. The settlers felt the land should belong to them! A treaty settled the problem. The Oregon country was divided. Great Britain was given Canada. Our northwest border became as it is today.

ACROSS THE COUNTRY TO THE FAR WEST

Each year more families began the long journey across the country. Some of the pioneers traveled over the Oregon Trail into the Northwest. Others traveled over the Santa Fe Trail into New Mexico and the Southwest. Others went across the Rocky Mountains into California. Most of the pioneers faced the same hardships and the same dangers. All of them had courage and brave hearts!

The story of the Preston family might help to picture the long and dangerous journey to the West.

 Mr. Preston called sharply to the oxen as they began to leave the rough trail. He put his hand on the wooden yoke about their necks and guided them back onto the path. Mrs. Preston, who was sitting in the covered wagon with her two small children, gave a sigh of relief.

All day the little caravan of covered wagons had traveled over roads thick with mud. If the wagons left the trail, a wheel might be broken or the wagon might become mired in the mud.

Mr. Preston smiled at his wife as the oxen took the trail again. He called to the two older boys, Jimmy and Robert. "Tomorrow the sun will shine," he said cheerfully.

The boys laughed. They did not mind the rain and the mud. That night the family all slept in the covered wagon. On clear nights the father and the two boys slept on the ground.

By morning the trail was drier. There were deep ruts where wagon wheels had sunk into the mud, but traveling was faster. At noon the little group met another caravan of wagons. There was much laughing and talking as the groups met. No one was far from home yet. They did not know the dangers they were to meet.

As the caravans began to move again, the wagons were driven in three columns. It was safer to travel this way. Before many days the "Indian country" would be reached. Many of the red men were friendly, but others often attacked the caravans. They set fire to the wagons. They captured the women and children. Sometimes they tortured the men or killed them.

As the days went by there were many strange experiences. One morning the caravan came to a stream of water. The men looked at the swiftly rushing water. Could they *ford* the stream by driving their wagons through it? Would they have to travel downstream until they found a shallow place to cross? Would they have to build rafts to take the caravan across?

233

"Bob," called Mr. Preston. "Bring Brownie here."

Bob went to the back of the wagon. The brown pony whinnied loudly as the boy walked toward her. Bob patted her gently on the head while he untied the rope that held her. Then he led her to his father.

"Brownie can swim," said Mr. Preston. "I'll ride her. If she can walk across the stream, the wagons can cross, too."

Mr. Preston urged the pony forward. Into the water they went. Everyone watched eagerly. The water was getting deeper. Would it be still deeper in the middle of the stream?

Presently there was a shout of joy. Brownie had walked across! Everyone climbed into the covered wagons. The men took the reins and drove the horses and oxen into the water. Soon every wagon was across and the journey was continued.

Night came. The wagons were driven into two large circles, an inner circle and an outer circle. The women began to cook supper over hastily built campfires. Children played inside the circles and ran in and out among the wagons.

It was good after a hard day's journey to eat, rest, and visit with the others. After supper the group sang for a while. The strains of lively music rang out on the lonely trail. Then the sweet music of an old hymn was sung.

Mothers began putting their children to bed in the covered wagons. Mr. Preston whispered to his wife. "It is my turn to stand guard tonight. The women and children are safe in the *inner* circle. I will stand with the men behind the wagons in the *outer* circle. If the Indians should attack, I can shoot and still be well protected by the wagons."

The Indians did not come, but in the morning the little group was sad. One of the women had been ill for many days. This morning she was too sick to be moved at all. The caravan decided to rest for the day. When the wagons moved on, a fresh grave marked the trail to the west.

Weeks went by. The little caravan moved more slowly. The men were tired from walking along with the cattle. The women were tired, too, and the children cried often.

The trail became hot and dusty. There was little water. Mothers whispered to their children. "Do not wet your lips. The hot wind will dry them. They will crack and bleed."

Bob and Jimmy walked along with their father. There was not much laughing or singing now. The little caravan was strangely quiet. Only the creaking of the wagons sounded as the group moved on to the west.

Late in the afternoon someone called, "Water, water!" In the distance was a stream of water. Men and boys walked more quickly. The women urged the horses and the oxen forward. Soon the people were all drinking the cooling water. Once more there was laughter and song on the trail.

But more days passed. The path became rugged and steep. Up, up, and up it went—into the mountains. At one place it suddenly dipped down. The party had come to a high cliff. *There*

235

was no roadway down the cliff! The men lowered the wagons with heavy ropes and the party went on.

Food supplies ran low. Many of the people had grown thin—many were ill. The Prestons had little food, but other families had none. They ate what the others shared with them. In the mountains it had been cold at night and hot in the daytime. But there had been water. There had been wild animals to kill for food.

Now the trail went slowly down the mountainside. A desert land of gray-green sagebrush stretched before the travelers. Again there would be no water! Again there would be little food!

The weary party moved on. Each day they traveled more slowly. Everyone was hungry. No one felt well. But on and on they struggled. One day a guide rode into camp. "There is a trading post a few miles away," he called.

Once more the people were filled with new hope. At the trading post they could buy food and other supplies. That night when the Preston family made camp, they all thanked God that the long journey to the West was nearly over!

It took brave men and women to make the long journey to the West. During the summer, the trip across the desert was almost unbearable. The blazing sun beat down mercilessly. Throats became dry and parched. As the people plodded along, it seemed that the desert would *never* end. Many of them did not live to cross it!

Other pioneers, trapped in the ice and snow of winter, suffered just as greatly. One party, called the *Donner Party*, started to cross the Sierra Nevada into California. It was late in the fall, but the people thought they had time to make the journey.

To their surprise, the winter storms broke early. The leaders begged the little party to hurry. Through blinding snowstorms and biting winds they struggled on. They reached the summit of the mountains near Donner Lake. But they could go no farther. Trapped in the snow, they were forced to spend the winter there.

It was a terrible winter! The families shared food as long as they had any. They ate the hides and bones of animals. They even ate mice that strayed into camp.

Many times they shoveled the snow off their tents and huts to keep from being buried alive. Sometimes the children could not get up in the morning until the snow had been shoveled off their beds. The people could not keep fires going. Most of them starved or froze to death.

Marcus Whitman led his party over the Rockies. He was one of the first missionaries to go to Oregon to teach the Indians.

Whitman built a mission and taught the Indians about Christianity. Later he was killed but he helped to open the Northwest.

Later on, pioneers went to the Northwest, too. Long trains of big covered wagons moved steadily over the Oregon Trail.

The pioneers began to settle the land, but they were not happy. The United States and England both claimed Oregon.

The pioneers felt the land should belong to them since they had built homes there. Great Britain felt the land was half hers.

The problem was settled by a treaty between England and the United States. Our northwest border became as it is today.

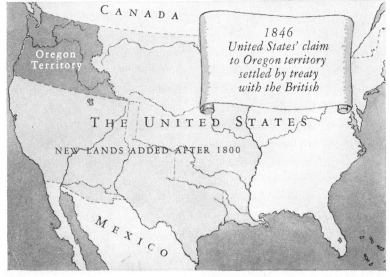

CANADA

Oregon Territory

1846
United States' claim to Oregon territory settled by treaty with the British

THE UNITED STATES

NEW LANDS ADDED AFTER 1800

MEXICO

Some of the westward moving pioneers belonged to the Church of Jesus Christ of Latter Day Saints, or the Mormon Church. The Mormon Church was begun in New York State, but the members soon moved from there. They went first to Ohio, later to Missouri, and then to Illinois. The people of Illinois welcomed them at first. Later they did not like some of the Mormon beliefs. They made the Mormons so unhappy the members were forced to move.

The leaders of the church decided to move to the West. They hoped to find freedom and peace on the frontier. They also hoped to find a place where they could worship God as they chose. In 1846 a party set out with its leader, Brigham Young, to find a place for a settlement.

The journey across the plains was very difficult. Many people were too poor to buy horses or oxen. They pushed or dragged their belongings in little handcarts.

On July 24, 1847, Brigham Young and his weary party came to the edge of the great Salt Lake Valley. They stopped on the narrow mountain trail overlooking the broad valley. Brigham Young turned to his waiting people. "This is the place," he said quietly.

For many days the Mormons had looked for a place to settle and build homes. When the people saw the place their leader had chosen, many of them were sick at heart. The wide valley was covered with nothing but sagebrush. There were miles and miles of desert. How could they build homes there?

But with a will the Mormons began to work. They set up tents, built sod and log houses, and began to plow the ground. They dug canals from the mountain streams to the farm lands. They turned the water from the mountain streams into the canals. The water flowed down the valley, through more ditches, and onto the farms.

This method of watering dry lands is called *irrigation*. The Mormons were the first people to *irrigate* the western desert.

After the Mormons learned to irrigate the land, the Salt Lake Valley was no longer a desert. More farms were laid out. Little towns were begun. More people came there to live. The state of *Utah* was being settled.

Members of the Mormon Church moved west in search of new homes and the right to worship God in the way they wished.

They endured many hardships. When they came to the Great Salt Lake Valley, they saw only barren desert and the waters of a lake.

Brigham Young, the leader of the little group, went to a bluff overlooking the valley. "This is the place," he said. "We will build homes!"

Some of the men wondered how they could build homes in the dry desert. But they set to work with a will and homes were soon built.

The Mormons brought water from mountain streams to irrigate their farms. The barren land became a desert garden.

After the Mormons learned to irrigate the dry land, more people went there to live. The state of Utah was being settled.

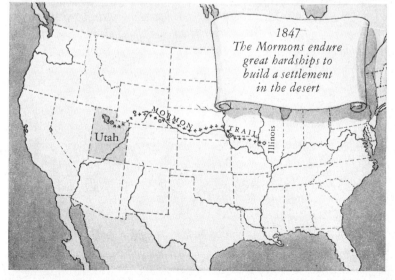

1847
The Mormons endure great hardships to build a settlement in the desert

MORMON TRAIL

Utah

Illinois

While California was still a part of Mexico, John Sutter owned a large tract of land in the Sacramento Valley. He built a fort and established a settlement there. One day he asked James Marshall to build a sawmill in the forest near the American River.

To provide water power for the mill, Marshall and his men built a dam across the river. Then they dug a ditch, or a canal, along the riverbank. The canal cut into the river above the dam and joined it again below the dam.

To control the water, a gate was built across the canal above the dam. The mill was then built near the canal so the flowing water would turn the mill wheel. The turning wheel furnished the power to operate the sawmill.

In January, 1848, *just before Mexico gave California to the United States,* some workmen were digging out the canal to make it deeper. Each morning they closed the control gate to hold back the water so the men could dig. Each evening they opened the gate so the rushing waters would carry away the loosened dirt.

One morning Marshall closed the gate to drain the canal. When the water had run off, he saw shining metal flakes among the rocks. *Could the shining yellow metal be gold?* Marshall gathered some of the flakes and tested them. "They *are* gold!" he told the men excitedly. "I am going down the mountain to tell Sutter."

Sutter and Marshall meant to keep the discovery of gold a secret, but the news leaked out. In 1849 people from all parts of the nation rushed to California, hoping to get rich. Because there were so many of them, 1849 was called the year of the great "gold rush." The men who went to California were called the *forty-niners.*

244

The forty-niners traveled up many little mountain streams looking for gold. They carried pickaxes and shovels over their shoulders as they trudged along the narrow trails. Beside them walked mules or pack horses loaded with provisions. Hanging from the packsaddles were pans for washing gold.

As soon as a good place was found, the forty-niner "pitched camp." Sometimes he slept in a tent, sometimes on the ground. During the day he *panned* for gold.

The forty-niner dipped a shallow pan into the stream and filled it with sand. Then he washed the sand away by dipping the pan into the water again and again. This left the grains of gold in the bottom of the pan. The miner put the grains of gold into a leather pouch, which hung around his neck. Then he went on panning for more gold.

A few men became rich. Others lost everything they had. It was a happy and an unhappy time! But after a while people realized that there was more than gold in California. Men turned to the rich, fertile soil to make a living. They laid out farms, vineyards, orange groves, and orchards.

In 1850 California became a state. The people planned a good government. There was law and order, and *California* became a good place in which to live.

From the Atlantic to the Pacific. Our country now reached from the Atlantic to the Pacific. Brave pioneers had journeyed across the country. They had built homes in the western wilderness. Most of them had lived in log cabins. All of them had raised their own food and made their own clothes. All of them had worked hard to find peace and happiness in a new land. All of them had helped to make our country as it is today.

245

In early California, priests and some of the Indians lived in the peaceful missions. Other people lived on small farms and ranches.

But the great rush to California did not begin until James Marshall discovered gold in a mill-race near the American River.

As soon as gold was discovered, people rushed to California. Some traveled by boat around South America and up the Pacific Coast.

So many men came in 1849 that they were called "forty-niners." They looked for gold in the many little mountain streams.

Then men discovered even greater treasure — the *soil*. They laid out farms, vineyards, and orchards in the fertile valleys.

California was a "fortune-hunting" state no longer. It became a state of farms and good homes. It joined the Union in 1850.

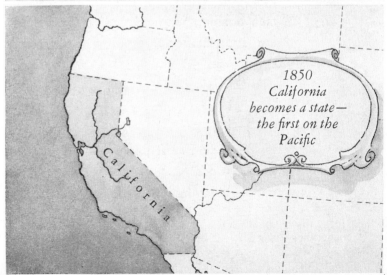

1850 California becomes a state— the first on the Pacific

THINGS TO DO

1. Collect pictures of pioneer scenes. Put them around your room and have a "pioneer day." Invite some other class to join you. Explain your pictures to your guests. Sing songs that were sung by the pioneers. Dance a square dance.

2. In some other book, find a story of life on the Santa Fe Trail. Tell the story to the class.

3. Draw scenes that will show some of the hardships suffered by the pioneers who settled the West.

4. Read more about the lives of Sam Houston, Stephen F. Austin, and Marcus Whitman. Read about other pioneer leaders. Tell the class the most interesting things you read.

5. Make a large outline map of the United States. Color the parts of the country that were now settled. One part of the country had not been settled. Leave that part white and mark it "Unsettled."

6. Read more about the way people lived in California during the "gold rush." Make a report to the class.

7. On a piece of paper write which of the following you would have seen if you had traveled over the trails to the West.

railroad stations	steep mountain trails
men panning for gold	electric lights
log schoolhouses	desert lands
streetcars	large cities
wild animals	little frontier villages
covered wagon caravans	people pushing handcarts
tall buildings	land being irrigated
Indians riding swift ponies	airplanes
paved roads	wagons fording streams
people going hungry	new farm lands

248

LET'S TALK ABOUT—

1. Why the men at the Alamo will always be remembered.

2. How the pioneers proved they had great courage.

3. How the lives of the colonists and the pioneers were alike.

4. Why the first pioneers suffered more hardships than the pioneers who came later.

5. Why the people who settled the Atlantic seacoast were called colonists. Why the people who settled the West were called pioneers.

NEW WORDS

The following words are used in the next story. Look up the meanings of any of these words you do not know. Then write a sentence using each word. Put any words you did not know in your word file.

sod	withdrawn	remove
seeped	survive	objected
reservation	encouraged	expensive
secede	representatives	congressmen	region

NAMES YOU WILL MEET IN THE NEXT STORY

Confederate States of America	Havana
Ulysses S. Grant	Puerto Rico
Alaska	Guam
Hawaiian Islands	Cuba

There were settlements on the eastern sea-board, as far west as the Mississippi Valley, and on the Pacific Coast. *But the country in between was not settled.* Before homes were built on the grassy plains and in the mountain regions, the young nation had a troubled time.

The people in the North and the people in the South had a serious quarrel. For a time it looked as if the United States might become two separate nations. But after the country was united again, pioneers settled on the Great Plains and in the mountain regions. Faraway lands were also added to our country.

After you have read this story, talk about how the country was nearly divided. Discuss how the Great Plains were settled. Talk about the faraway lands that we gained.

OUR COUNTRY GROWS STILL LARGER

Each day the pioneers were adding new territory to the United States. Each day the nation seemed to be growing stronger and stronger. But while this was happening, the North and the South were drifting apart. The quarrel that grew up between them weakened and almost destroyed the Union.

THE NORTH AND THE SOUTH DISAGREE

Most of the southerners owned large plantations. Many of the northerners owned or worked in factories and stores. The needs of the two were quite different.

In the North there were more people than there were in the South. This gave the northerners more representatives in Congress. The northern congressmen passed laws that made the southern planters angry. "The laws help the North and hurt the South," the planters protested.

The North and the South also disagreed about slavery. Slaves were not needed in the northern factories. The northerners thought all the slaves should be freed. The southern planters needed the slaves. They felt the government had no right to tell them what to do.

At that time Abraham Lincoln was a young lawyer in Illinois. He felt very deeply about the question of slavery. In one of his speeches he declared that the nation could not survive "half slave and half free."

When Lincoln ran for president, the southern planters were worried. "What will happen if he is elected?" they asked one another. "If Lincoln becomes president, perhaps we should leave the Union and form our own government."

When Lincoln became president, the South *did* leave the Union. Seven southern states started a new nation. They called it the *Confederate States of America*. Later, four other southern states joined the Confederacy.

TROUBLED TIMES

The men who sat around the long mahogany table looked very grave. None of them smiled. Most of them stared straight ahead. In the eyes of some of the men burned a fierce anger. The tall, thin man at the head of the table was grave, too. Yet his eyes held an expression of sympathy and kindness.

President Abraham Lincoln looked at the men seated around him. "It is a serious time," he said solemnly. "We must act. But we must act wisely if we are to bring the southern states back into the Union.

"I can well understand the feelings of the southerners. They need the Negroes to help them with their work. But I have been elected President of the United States. *I do not believe that any state has the right to secede.*

"From my point of view the southern states are still a part of the nation. It is my duty to enforce the national laws there. It is my duty to protect United States property in the South as well as in any of the other states."

"The leaders in the South do not think so," said one of the men quickly. "They believe that any property within the limits of the state belongs to the state."

"Yes, I know," answered President Lincoln. "For that reason they insisted that Fort Sumter, on an island near Charleston, belonged to South Carolina. They demanded that the soldiers in the fort surrender. When they heard that I was sending a supply ship to help the men, they decided to attack at once. They forced the United States soldiers in the fort to surrender."

A shadow seemed to cloud President Lincoln's face. "They hauled down the American flag," he said quietly. "The Confederate flag now flies over the fort."

"What will you do, Mr. President?"

"I shall ask Congress to declare war. Not because I wish to fight against our southern brothers, but because I wish to bring them back into the Union. *Our nation cannot survive if it is divided.*"

THE WAR BETWEEN THE STATES

The attack on Fort Sumter brought on a war between the states. The people in the North were very angry. "The American flag has been fired upon!" they cried. "We must fight to preserve the Union." Many men offered to serve in the northern army.

It was a troubled time for the nation! Each side was fighting for what it believed to be right. Most northerners believed there should be no slaves. They believed that no state had the right to withdraw from the Union.

Most of the southerners believed they should have the right to make their own laws regarding slavery. They believed that each new state should have the right to allow slavery or to forbid it.

There were bitter feelings on both sides. Many of the people in the North believed that every slaveholder was cruel and unjust. The southerners believed that their freedom was being taken away from them.

THE SLAVES ARE FREED

President Lincoln did not like slavery, but he felt that his first duty was to bring the southern states back into the Union. Later he decided that "slavery must die that the Union may live."

The slaves were raising food for the Confederate army. They were hauling supplies and helping to build forts. At one time it looked as if the slaves might help their masters win the war.

On *January 1, 1863*, President Lincoln signed a paper declaring that the slaves in the Confederate states were free. This paper is called the *Emancipation Proclamation*.

THE WAR GOES ON

For four long years the war went on. General Ulysses S. Grant was commander of the northern armies. General Robert E. Lee led the southern armies. There were many battles. Sometimes the South won; sometimes the North.

But, as the months went by, the southern armies grew smaller and smaller. They became ragged and hungry. At last, in April, 1865, General Lee was forced to surrender.

General Grant wrote out the terms of surrender: all guns, wagons, cannons, and property belonging to the Confederate government were to be turned over to the United

States. The men were to keep their horses and personal property. General Lee thanked Grant for allowing the men to keep their horses.

"They will need them for the spring plowing," said Grant.

When General Grant returned to his waiting soldiers, they began to cheer. General Grant stopped them. "The southerners are our countrymen again," he said simply.

The war was over. The northern soldiers soon found work in the busy mills and factories. But the war had been fought in the South. Southern towns and cities had been burned. Growing crops had been destroyed. Railroads had been torn up.

The South faced a difficult task. But, as the years went by, the southern towns and cities were rebuilt. Peaceful times came again. Once more the southern states were prosperous and happy.

ABRAHAM LINCOLN—A WISE, KIND PRESIDENT

Abraham Lincoln was born in a tiny log cabin in Kentucky on February 12, 1809. His family was very poor. When he was seven, his father moved the family to Indiana. Their first winter there was very difficult. They lived in a three-sided hut that opened to the south. On the open

side a fire was kept burning night and day. Even then the children were often cold.

During that winter Lincoln's mother died. A few years later his father married again. The new stepmother, Sarah Lincoln, was very good to young Abe. She encouraged him to study and to do well.

When school was held in the little log schoolhouse, she saw that young Lincoln attended. But school was not held often. Abraham Lincoln went to school less than a year. But he taught himself to do sums in arithmetic, to spell, and to speak and to write good English.

When he was twenty-one his family moved to Illinois. After that Lincoln did many things. He kept a store, fought in an Indian war, surveyed land, and studied law.

In 1837 he went to Springfield, Illinois, to practice law. He won many cases in court. He also won many friends. Everyone seemed to like this tall, kindly man who told funny stories and did good deeds.

When he was president, he wanted more than anything else to save the Union. He lived to see the nation united. But soon afterwards he was shot while he was watching a play in Ford's Theater in Washington.

His friends carried him to a house across the street, and many men came to honor him. *But Lincoln died without knowing that the world would love and honor his name!*

In the morning the sad news spread throughout the nation. Overnight the country had lost one of its greatest leaders—the South, its kindest friend.

GENERAL ROBERT E. LEE

Robert E. Lee was born two years before Lincoln, on January 19, 1807. His boyhood life was very different from that of young Lincoln. Lee grew up in a comfortable Virginia home and was taught by private tutors.

When he was eighteen, he was appointed to West Point. After he graduated, he served in the United States Army for many years. Then came word that the southern states had withdrawn from the Union. It was an unhappy time for Lee! He loved his country and all it stood for, but he also loved his home and his state.

When the war began, Lee was offered command of the Union armies. He refused. "I cannot lead an army against the people of my own state," he said sadly.

Lee returned home and took command of the soldiers in Virginia. He did not want to fight against the northern armies. He wanted only to protect the people of his beloved state. But the South called him to command all of the Confederate forces.

General Lee was a wise commander, but the northern armies were too strong. Lee was forced to surrender. After the surrender he returned to his men with a sad heart. "I have done the best I could for you," he said quietly. "We must now rebuild the South. The people of the South must join hands with the people of the North. They must work together as brothers. That is the only way we can make our country really united."

After the war, Lee became president of Washington College at Lexington, Virginia. He spent the last five years of his life there. To honor him, the name of the school was changed to Washington and Lee University.

Southerners felt they needed Negroes to work on their plantations. Northerners thought the Negroes should be free.

Southerners were afraid their rights would be taken from them. They left the Union and set up the Confederate States of America.

Lincoln said the South could not withdraw. War was declared and many Northerners joined the army to *save the Union.*

Lincoln's first thought, too, was to save the Union. But later he signed the *Emancipation Proclamation*, freeing all the slaves.

Four years after war began, General Lee surrendered to General Grant. Once again the North and the South became one nation.

With all the states again united, the people once more worked together. The country began to grow and prosper.

Growth and progress in a nation again united

Our country was at peace. The people in the North and the people in the South were friends again. While they were at war, only a few pioneers moved to the West. But now that the war was over, the trails to the West were crowded again.

Early in the story of our country, the frontier was moved west to the Ohio Valley. Then it was pushed west to the Mississippi. From there it was pushed farther and farther west. Then came stories of the rich soil in Oregon and the discovery of gold in California. People rushed to the Pacific Coast. They forgot all about the grassy land of the Great Plains. But after the war the Great Plains were finally settled.

Roaming across the plains of Texas and the Southwest were large herds of wild cattle. The herds had been started by the Spanish rancheros. The Americans caught the wild animals and branded them.

Each cattle owner had a brand, or a mark. The brand was burned into the flesh of the animal with a hot branding iron. Then nothing could remove it. This helped the rancher claim his cattle no matter where they strayed.

When the miners in California began to find less and less gold, they went to other mountain regions. They found gold and other precious metals in Oregon, Washington, Idaho, Nevada, Montana, and Colorado. They started little mining towns there. The miners did not want to farm the soil. They wanted to get rich quickly.

The western miners and the people in the East needed food. The ranchers in Texas had plenty of cattle. But it was a long way to the mining towns in the West and the factory towns in the East. During the long journey the cattle became thin, and the ranchers lost money.

In time the Texas ranchers began to drive their cattle north to the grassy lands of the Great Plains. The cattle roamed over the plains and grew fat on the rich green grass. Then they were sent to market.

A man who owned cattle was called a *rancher*. The men who herded and tended the cattle were called *cowboys*. For a number of years the cowboys and their herds roamed over the Great Plains. Then Congress passed a law called the *Homestead Act*. This law gave 160 acres of land to any person who would build a home and live on the land for five years.

On the Great Plains were acres and acres of good land. Farmers began moving into the plains country. At first there were many disputes between the farmers and the ranchers. But little by little the herds of cattle were driven west into the mountains.

HOMES ON THE PRAIRIES

Most of the pioneers who moved to the West found great forests. They cleared the forests and built log cabins. The early pioneers who settled on the prairies had quite a different problem. The prairie land was covered with tall, thick grass. The roots of the grass were deeply matted in the rich black soil.

The prairie settler had little to work with. The only trees to be found were those growing near a stream of water. The settler could not find lumber—he had to use the *land* to build his home.

He cut saplings at the nearest river and hauled them across the prairie by oxen. Then he turned over the rich prairie soil and cut blocks of sod from the grassy land. The blocks of sod were piled one upon the other—row after row. Each row made the walls of the house a little higher. When the sod walls were high enough, the settler laid the saplings across the walls to form a support for the roof.

Then he put a layer of sod upon the saplings. He laid the sod blocks very close together so the roof would be tight. Even then the water seeped through when it rained!

When he began his journey west, the settler sometimes packed a glass window and a wooden door in one corner of his covered wagon. When he reached the prairies he was very proud. The window and the door made his cabin a little nicer than the others. After he whitewashed the walls of his sod house, it began to seem like a home.

But some of the settlers were not so fortunate! Scattered over the rich farm lands were homes little better than caves. In these crude homes the floor of the house was about four feet below the ground. The sod walls rose but a few feet above the ground.

There was one window in the house, but it was not made of glass nor covered with oiled paper. It was a hole in the sod wall. In the summertime it was left open. In the winter it was covered with a heavy blanket.

But as soon as the settlers had plowed the prairies and planted crops, little villages were begun. In the villages were houses with log walls and sod roofs. There were even a few log cabins. The richer settlers brought logs from the riverbanks to build their houses.

The settler in the country went to the village to buy calico, gunpowder, flour, sugar, and salt, and to receive his mail from the village storekeeper.

The children who lived on the prairie farms went to

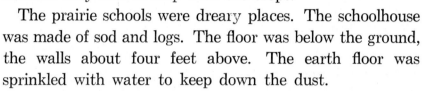

school in the village. Most of the schools were open only three months in the summer. In the winter the boys and girls could not struggle through the deep snows. In the spring and fall they had to help with the crops.

The prairie schools were dreary places. The schoolhouse was made of sod and logs. The floor was below the ground, the walls about four feet above. The earth floor was sprinkled with water to keep down the dust.

The desks in the schoolhouse were split logs with the flat side up. They rested on crude wooden legs or on stout sticks. The benches were like the desks only not so high. At the front of the room was the teacher's desk. It was made very tall so the teacher could watch the boys and girls as they worked.

The pupils brought to school any books they happened to have at home. Sometimes each pupil in the room had a different book. A few of the prairie boys and girls learned to read from the *New England Primer*.

The teacher cut pens from goose feathers and gave the older pupils writing lessons. The younger pupils wrote on slates. The boys and girls learned to read, write, spell, sing, and work problems in arithmetic.

The schoolmaster boarded with the parents of the pupils. Every week or two he moved from one home to another. He was paid with chickens, pigs, corn, hams, or anything the settler could spare. The schoolmaster traded these things at the village store for whatever he needed.

In the evening the grown-up people often gathered in the little schoolhouses. Home-dipped candles lighted the room as the people sang, had spelling matches, and played games. It was a happy time for all!

In 1849 the great "gold rush" in California took place. There were also "land rushes." As our country grew larger, new regions of land were added. Some of the new lands were public lands. They belonged to the government.

When the Homestead Act was passed, the government opened up many of the new lands. When new land was opened up there was often a "land rush." One large land rush took place in the territory that is now Oklahoma.

●

The long-awaited day had finally come. People moved restlessly along the border line. Nearly twenty thousand of them waited for the new lands to be opened.

There were people in covered wagons, in carriages, on horses, and on foot. For hours and hours they had camped along the border. For hours and hours they had talked of nothing but the new land. It was said to be the richest in the country!

Each man waited anxiously. When the signal came he wanted to get a good start. He wanted to rush ahead of the others and claim the finest land.

Guards walked up and down the border. Occasionally they pushed a wagon back into line. They spoke sharply to men who were fighting and quarreling.

Twelve o'clock drew near. The men picked up the reins of their horses. They wanted to be ready at a moment's notice! All eyes were turned toward an officer on horseback. The officer rode to the highest point of ground near the border and held up a flag.

Twelve o'clock came! The officer gave a signal to the waiting people. The new lands were opened!

As the signal was given, the people rushed forward. They raced madly for land in the new territory. Each man hoped to claim the finest and best land in Oklahoma.

●

Many of the people farmed the land and built homes. Others claimed the land so they could sell it later. But there was one thing all the people wanted—they wanted to improve their ways of living.

264

THE INDIAN FINDS A NEW HOME

The story of the white man's march to the West was an unhappy story for the Indian. He could not understand the white man's way of living. He could not understand why the settlers killed the buffalo. He could not understand why they cleared the forests and built homes. He could not understand why towns and cities were built on lands that had long belonged to his ancestors.

Many of the red men fought stubbornly to keep their lands. But the white men were stronger. They needed the land for homes. As time went on, the Indians were forced to give up more and more of their hunting grounds.

The government made treaties with the Indians, and much of the Indian land was bought and paid for. But the Indians who sold their homes had no place to go. They had no homes. They had no way of making a living.

To help the Indians, the government set aside lands for them to live on. These lands are called *reservations*. A few of the Indians were given land of their own, but most of them now live on the reservations.

265

As the pioneers moved west they made many trails over the prairies. But they did not stop to settle on the Great Plains.

Then ranchers from Texas and the Southwest drove their cattle onto the plains. The cattle ate the green grass and grew fat.

At first the ranchers had the land to themselves. Then the Homestead Act was passed. Farmers moved in and built new homes.

266

There were few trees on the plains. Early settlers had to cut blocks of sod and use them for building their houses.

The cattlemen did not like to have the farmers move in. There were many disputes, but the ranchers were forced back to the mountains.

As time went on, the farmers raised crops, planted trees, and built better homes. Prairie life became more pleasant!

Our country had grown from the Atlantic to the Pacific. Now it grew still larger. As the years went by, new lands were added—new lands that were far away.

When the government talked of buying Alaska from the Russians, many people objected. *"The United States should not buy Alaska. Let the Russians keep it. The land has little value. It is nothing but an icebox."* But in 1867 Alaska was bought for $7,200,000.

The Alaskan country proved to be rich in natural resources. Furs, gold, silver, lead, copper, and coal were found there. Fertile soil, great forests, and plenty of fish were also found. The land proved to be worth far more than we paid for it!

Alaska is now a territory of the United States, but the people have applied for statehood.

The Hawaiian Islands are also a part of our country. These islands lie about two thousand miles west of California. The climate, the green mountains, the fertile valleys, the flowers, and the tangled forests make them one of the most beautiful places in the world.

More than one hundred years ago missionaries went to the islands to teach the natives. A little later, settlers followed the missionaries. The settlers bought land and raised sugar cane and pineapples. In time the Americans and many of the other people who lived on the islands asked to belong to the United States.

In 1900 Congress voted to make Hawaii one of our territories. Hawaii, too, has asked for statehood.

A war also added new lands to the United States. Cuba is an island about ninety miles from Florida. For a long time the people of Cuba were under the rule of Spain. But the Cubans were very unhappy. They tried again and again to win their independence.

Finally Spain sent a very stern general to Cuba. This made the Cubans want their freedom more than ever. The Americans on the island were unhappy, too. They asked the United States to protect their lives and their property.

About the time Hawaii was annexed, the United States sent a warship, the *Maine*, to Cuba. The *Maine* was blown up in the harbor of Havana. The Spaniards claimed they did not blow up the ship, but war followed. The United States won the war in less than four months.

After the war, the islands of Cuba, Puerto Rico, Guam, and the Philippines came under our control. Cuba was given her full freedom. Later, the people in the Philippines were also allowed to rule themselves. Puerto Rico, Guam, and other little islands scattered throughout the oceans still belong to the United States.

When our government talked of buying Alaska, people said the land had little value. But we bought it in 1867 for $7,200,000.

We soon found the country was rich in natural resources. The land has proved far more valuable than the price we paid for it.

Hawaii was also added to our country. The people rebelled against native rule and formed a government of their own.

Not long after, they asked the United States to annex the islands. In 1900 Congress voted to make Hawaii one of our territories.

The *Maine* was sent to Spanish Cuba to protect Americans living on the island. The ship was blown up. War with Spain followed.

In less than four months we won the war. After the war, many islands in different parts of the world came under our control.

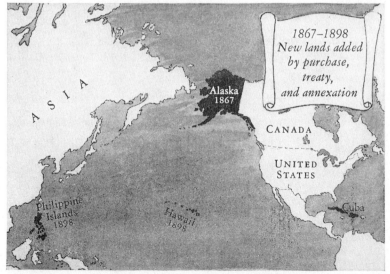

1867–1898
New lands added by purchase, treaty, and annexation

ASIA

Alaska 1867

CANADA

UNITED STATES

Philippine Islands 1898

Hawaii 1898

Cuba

The Panama Canal is another possession of the United States—a very important possession. For many years men had dreamed of joining the Atlantic and Pacific oceans. Even the early explorers realized that many miles of travel would be saved if there were a waterway from the Atlantic to the Pacific.

But such a waterway was not found, and for years men did little but dream. They knew that if a waterway connected the two oceans, the journey from the east coast to the west coast would not be so long. It would not be so dangerous. But how could they make their dream come true? Engineers studied the problem. Finally they gave their answer. *If a canal could be built through the Isthmus of Panama, the two oceans would be connected!*

Not long after the War between the States, the French tried to build such a canal. But they found it very expensive. In addition, so many of their workmen died from yellow fever that they finally gave up the idea.

Then the United States government bought the interests of the French in the canal. It also leased a strip of land ten miles wide across Panama. This strip is called the *Canal Zone*. The United States gave Panama ten million dollars for the use of the land. It also agreed to pay Panama $250,000 (later $430,000) a year after the first nine years.

In 1904 the United States began building the canal. The first task was to make the country safe for the workers. By this time, doctors had learned that yellow fever and malaria are spread by the bite of the mosquito.

The first two years of building the canal were spent in cleaning up the land. Swamps were cleared and drained. Oil was spread on ponds and streams where mosquitoes

272

might breed. Hospitals were built to take care of the sick. Health programs were begun to teach the people how to stay well and how to take care of themselves.

After this the real work of digging the canal began. Engineers decided to build a canal with *locks* instead of one at sea level. This meant that the completed canal was to be a "bridge of water." But the task of building it was tremendous.

Slowly and with great difficulty workmen dug their way through a huge mountain ridge. They moved tons and tons of dirt. They built great locks and a large lake. Finally the giant task was finished.

The canal cost the United States nearly $400,000,000. But the government charges a toll for each ship that passes through the canal. During one twenty-year period, ships paid tolls that amounted to nearly half a billion dollars.

The Panama Canal is important to the national defense of the United States. But it is even more important to world shipping. The canal has helped not only our nation, but all the nations of the world.

A Time of Great Changes. Our country was settled from the Atlantic to the Pacific. We had gained lands in many parts of the world. What would Americans do now? What were they doing while our country was growing larger?

The American people have always wanted to find better ways of living. They have always tried to improve upon the things they had. While our country was growing larger, the people were seeking new and better ways of living.

They made many changes in our way of life—changes that made life more pleasant and worth while. The next part of the book is the story of these changes. It is the story of how our nation became as it is today.

France tried to build a canal across the Isthmus of Panama but failed. The United States bought the interests of the French.

We also leased a strip of land ten miles wide across Panama to give us room to work. The strip is called the *Canal Zone.*

In 1904 we began to build the canal. But swamps had to be cleared and oil spread on ponds to kill the malaria mosquitoes.

Hospitals were built for the men who became sick. The well people were taught to protect themselves from the heat and malaria.

Then the task of digging the canal began. Slowly the workmen dug through a large mountain ridge. They moved tons of earth.

They built big locks to raise and lower the water level in the canal so ships could easily travel from one ocean to the other.

THINGS TO DO

1. Read more about the life of a cowboy. Tell the class some of the things the cowboys did that you would enjoy doing.

2. Make a large outline map of the United States. Cut the map into large pieces that will represent the different regions of our country that were settled by the colonists and the pioneers. Number your pieces. Make number 1 the first land that was settled. Make number 2 the second section of land that was settled. Do the same with each of your pieces. Then put the pieces together and tell, or write, a little story about each part of the map.

3. Make a model of a sod house.

4. Read more about the life of Abraham Lincoln. Tell stories that will show why he was a great man. Do the same with General Robert E. Lee.

5. Read more about the lands that belong to the United States. Collect pictures that will show how the people live. Make charts that will tell the story of our possessions.

6. Find pictures of the Panama Canal. Read more about how it was built and how the locks operate.

LET'S TALK ABOUT—

1. Why the Great Plains were settled last and who settled there.

2. Why the first pioneers on the prairies built sod houses, and why the sod houses were good houses for the prairies.

3. The difference between a land rush and a gold rush.

4. Why Abraham Lincoln wanted to bring the southern states back into the Union.

5. How we gained our lands outside the United States.

NEW WORDS

The following words are used in the next story. Some of them may be new to you. Look up any of these words you do not know. Talk about them in class. Let the class write sentences using each word. Put in your word file the words you did not know.

gradually   glider   experiments

magnet   assistant   corduroy

cable   instruments

NAMES YOU WILL MEET IN THE NEXT STORY

Conestoga wagons   John McAdam   Schenectady

Promontory Point   Alfred Vail   Cyrus W. Field

Samuel F. B. Morse   Alexander Graham Bell Marconi

Pathfinders blaze trails to the west.

At the Alamo, Texans fight for freedom.

Westward-moving settlers float down the Ohio.

Missionaries teach Indians of Oregon.

Settlers clear forests and plant crops.

Many pioneers move into Oregon Territory.

Lewis and Clark explore the Northwest.

Mormon settlers build homes in Utah.

Gold brings settlers to California.

President Lincoln frees the slaves.

Ranchers drive cattle to Great Plains.

Alaska is purchased from Russia.

Farmers build homes on the prairies.

Hawaii becomes a part of our country.

Northerners enlist to save Union.

United States builds Panama Canal.

Daniel Boone makes his first trip to Kentucky　　1767
Spanish priests build missions in California

The Declaration of Independence is signed　　1776

George Washington becomes our first president　　1789
Jefferson becomes president

Louisiana is purchased　　1803
Lewis and Clark explore new northwest territory
Settlers move farther west to build new homes

Whitman builds a mission at Walla Walla　　1836
The battle of the Alamo is fought
Texas becomes a free republic

Texas is admitted to the United States　　1845
The Oregon boundary dispute is settled
Mormon settlers build homes in Utah
Mexico gives southwestern lands to the United States

Gold is discovered in California　　1848
California becomes a state
The Gadsden Purchase is made
Oregon becomes a state

Abraham Lincoln is elected president　　1860
Southern states withdraw from the Union
Northern states fight to preserve the Union

The Homestead Act is passed　　1862
Settlers build homes on the prairies
Lincoln frees the slaves

The nation is again united　　1865
Alaska is purchased from Russia

The first transcontinental railroad is completed　　1869
The French start to build a canal in Panama
The Oklahoma land rush occurs

Hawaii becomes part of our country　　1898
A treaty with Spain adds new lands

The Panama Canal is built　　1904-1914

ALASKA

UNITED STATES MAINLAND

HAWAIIAN ISLANDS

PUERTO RICO

As the years passed, the United States became larger and larger. Today, our country includes the United States mainland, Alaska, Hawaii, Puerto Rico, the Canal Zone, and several islands in the Atlantic and Pacific.

W. C. M.

Part IV—OUR COUNTRY GROWS UP

Our nation was no longer thirteen states along the Atlantic seaboard. It was forty-eight states that reached from the Atlantic to the Pacific. It included new lands in far-away places. The stars and stripes flew proudly in many parts of the world.

While the nation was growing larger, other changes were also taking place. As soon as the people had settled the land, they wanted better ways of working and living. Men began to invent new and improved machinery. They invented many other things that helped to make your life as it is today.

After you have read this story, talk about how our ways of living changed. Talk about how the changes made our life more pleasant.

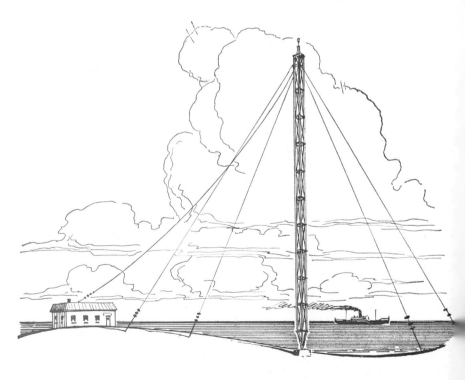

BETTER WAYS OF
TRAVEL AND COMMUNICATION

BUILDING BETTER ROADS

The colonial woman lifted her long, full skirts just a little. She stepped carefully over the puddles of mud on the sidewalk. As she heard the carriage come down the street, she moved as far away from the road as possible. Even then her dress was splattered with mud as the carriage and the horses splashed down the street.

In colonial times, the dirt roads and the sidewalks were mud puddles when it rained. They were rough and dusty in dry weather. The roads to the West were old Indian trails and buffalo paths. But the American people have always wanted better ways of living. They improved their homes, their food, and their clothes. Then they began to build better roads and better sidewalks.

In Philadelphia, cobblestone streets were built while Benjamin Franklin still lived. The cobblestone streets were much better than the old dirt roads and before long other towns and cities were building them, too. They were also paving their streets with bricks or wooden blocks.

The wooden blocks were set in thick mud. When the mud dried, it held the blocks in place. But the block roads were not successful. In one city a very heavy rainstorm washed away the dirt between the wooden blocks. As the storm cleared, the astonished people saw the wooden blocks floating down the street!

285

In 1794 the first hard-surface road in the United States was built. It was built from Philadelphia to Lancaster, Pennsylvania, and was called the *Lancaster Pike*. For many years the Lancaster Pike was considered the wonder of the East. People from many miles around came to ride over its hard surface of crushed rock.

A little later Congress voted money to build a road that would connect the East and the West. The first part of the road was built from Cumberland, Maryland, to Wheeling, West Virginia. This road was called the *Cumberland Road*, or the *National Road*.

Building the Cumberland Road was a difficult task. Trees were cut from a strip nearly sixty feet wide. In the middle of the strip a roadbed about twenty feet wide was cleared and leveled off. Then the road was covered with a layer of crushed stone.

But people soon learned how to improve the Cumberland Road. It became a wide road that sloped down at the sides to carry away the water. It was covered with crushed rock and then pressed with a heavy roller to make it smooth and hard. This type of road is called a macadam road. It was named for John McAdam, a Scotch engineer, who showed the people how to build it.

Along the Cumberland Road were many little toll stations. At the toll station a long pole was swung across the road to stop the travelers. When a traveler stopped, he was asked to pay a *toll*, or a certain sum of money, for traveling over the road. When the toll was paid, the traveler could continue his journey.

The Cumberland Road was gradually built farther and farther west. But in early times the first pioneers found traveling very difficult. Most of the western roads were rocky trails filled with big holes and deep ruts. In some

286

places the pioneers built corduroy roads but these roads were little better. A corduroy road was made by placing logs very close together across the roadway.

Charles Dickens, an English writer, describes his journey over one of the old corduroy roads in these words:

"At one time we were all flung together in a heap at the bottom of the coach, and at another we were crushing our heads against the roof. Now one side was down deep in the mire, and we were holding on to the other. The very slightest jolts with which the carriage fell from log to log seemed enough to break every bone in the human body."

It is no wonder the people wanted to improve their roads!

Before long the people in the West began building macadam roads. But soon men learned how to improve these roads. Melted tar was poured upon crushed rock. Then it was rolled with a heavy roller.

"We now have the finest road that can be built," said the people. But they were wrong. A little later concrete highways were built with cement, sand, and gravel.

Today modern highways lead to every part of our country. They wind over the mountains and across the deserts. They lead to the smallest towns and cities. How different they are from the old Indian trails of early America!

In colonial days, people walking on the sidewalk were often covered with mud as the horses splashed down the street.

Cobblestone, brick, and wooden pavements were built later. They did not become muddy, but they were very rough.

A little later a hard surface of crushed rock was spread on some roads. Toll stations were built and travelers paid a fee.

The pioneers built corduroy roads by laying logs very close together in the roadway. The road was very bumpy, but dry.

Then came macadam roads, named for John McAdam. They were covered with crushed rock and then pressed with a heavy roller.

Today macadam roads have been improved. Paved highways, broad and smooth, lead to nearly every part of the nation.

The first means of traveling in America were little better than the early roads. Some of the colonists used two-wheeled carts with heavy wooden wheels. Horses or plodding oxen pulled the crude carts that bumped and rattled along the rough trails.

Other colonists had light carriages that could easily be drawn by one horse. At first the light carriage was called a chaise. Later the people began to call it a shay, or a "one-hoss" shay.

Heavy carriages were also used in the colonies. They were called chariots and were drawn by four horses. The richer people often rode to church in their chariots.

Then the colonists began to build stagecoaches and heavy wagons. The stagecoaches were used to carry people from one town to another. Companies owned stage lines just as companies own railroad or bus lines today. The stages ran between all the important towns. Sometimes the driver of a stagecoach started as early as three o'clock in the morning so he would reach the next town the same day.

Four horses usually pulled the stagecoaches. The horses were changed about every twelve miles at places called "stages" or stations. The driver rested only at night.

It was not easy to drive a stagecoach over the rough roads. The driver had to be ready for any kind of trouble. If the stage got stuck in the mud, he and the passengers had to push it back on the road again. If it got stuck going up a hill, they had to push it up the hill.

Some of the passengers rode inside the stage. Others rode up on top with the driver. The baggage was carried on top of the stage or tied on the back of it.

The stagecoaches carried mail and passengers. The freight was usually hauled in heavy wagons called *Conestoga* wagons. The bed of the Conestoga wagon was lower in the middle than it was at each end. This kept the freight from slipping out.

The wagons were covered over with white canvas tops. The body of the wagon was painted blue and the sideboards bright red. From four to seven horses pulled the wagons. The driver rode on one of the front horses to guide the team. As the horses jogged along, the bells on their harness jingled loudly and merrily.

The wagons were used both in the East and in the West. Many of the pioneers traveled to the West in the Conestoga wagons. Welcome supplies for the little frontier towns and the trading posts were also hauled across the country in the big covered wagons.

Then came a change! For many years men had been trying to make a "carriage that would run without horses." A few had been made in Europe, but they had not been successful. Then men in the United States learned how to make gasoline from oil. Not long after this they learned to make an engine that would burn gasoline. The next step was a car run by a gasoline engine.

The first automobiles were not like those of today. They could travel little faster than a man could walk! They had no tops. As they chugged along over the rough roads, clouds of dust rolled up and almost choked the riders.

But both roads and automobiles have been improved. Today thousands and thousands of streamlined cars travel swiftly over our paved highways.

One way to travel in the colonies was by chaise, or "one-hoss shay." This was a two-wheeled cart pulled by a horse.

Stagecoaches were used to carry people from one town to another. In the early days they also carried the mail.

The freight was carried in Conestoga wagons. The pioneers also traveled to the West in the big canvas-covered wagons.

Then the first automobile was built. Men learned to make gasoline from oil. The day of "horseless carriages" was beginning.

By 1915, automobiles were a common sight on the roads. They had been improved and were faster and more comfortable riding.

Today, cars and trucks are streamlined for fast, comfortable travel. They are far different from colonial "shays" and coaches.

It was August 9, 1831. The *De Witt Clinton* was to make its first run from Albany to Schenectady, New York. As the train stood waiting on the tracks, crowds of people gathered around to look at it.

Behind the funny little engine was a car called the *tender*. The engineer stood on a platform at the rear of the tender. Behind the tender was a small flatcar for carrying wood and water. Next came three cars that looked like stagecoaches and several flatcars with plain wooden benches. The people rode in the coaches and on the flatcars.

Everyone waited anxiously for the beginning of the seventeen-mile journey. At last the whistle blew! The people on the train and the people standing beside the tracks began to cheer.

As the train began to move, there was a great jar. The tender and the cars were fastened together with chains. As the train started, the cars jerked and slammed against each other. Each jerk sent passengers onto the floor.

After the train got under way it ran more smoothly. But great clouds of smoke began to pour from the chimney of the engine. Then a shower of sparks from the wood-burning engine settled over the train. The people choked and coughed. They shook their clothing to brush off the sparks before it caught fire!

After the train had gone a few miles it stopped to take on water. Once more the chains jerked the cars! Again people were on the floor! The men on the train got off and took some rails from a nearby fence. They put the rails between the cars and tied them in place. When the train started again, the cars did not jerk.

A large crowd had gathered in Schenectady to see the

294

train come in. As the engine puffed down the track the people cheered. Men threw their hats in the air. Women waved handkerchiefs. *A train had run seventeen miles!*

As the pioneers moved west, the railroads pushed west, too. Then men dreamed of a railroad that would run across the country. The Union Pacific began to build tracks to the West. The Central Pacific in California started to build toward the East.

The government offered each company land and money, but building the railroad was a difficult task. Food, clothing, supplies, rails, and even some of the wooden ties had to be hauled great distances. But as the days went by, mile after mile of the iron rails were laid. On May 10, 1869, the rails were joined at Promontory Point, Utah.

The train from the East stood puffing on the eastern side of the tracks. The train from the West stood on the western tracks. People got off both of the trains. They laughed, talked, and shook hands heartily.

Then suddenly they became quiet. Heads were bowed and a prayer of thanks was offered. Then a number of men stepped forward. One large spike was left to be driven into the rails that joined the East and the West.

The large spike was made of gold. One man held the golden spike in place while other men drove it into the rail. *A railroad now crossed the country!*

The trains that met at Promontory Point were not like the first trains in America. They were larger and easier riding. The cars were closed in with glass windows. The plush seats were soft and comfortable.

But even those trains would look very old-fashioned today. Engines have been made larger and more powerful. The trains have been streamlined. People riding on the trains of today enjoy many comforts they have at home.

The Tom Thumb, one of the first trains in America to be run by steam, raced a horse-drawn car down the tracks. The train won.

Another early train, the De Witt Clinton, made its first run on August 9, 1831. It ran for seventeen miles — going from Albany to Schenectady.

After trains were improved, people wanted a railroad that would cross the country. Men began to build a transcontinental railway.

Trains from the East and West met at Promontory Point, Utah. A gold spike was driven in the rails to complete the railway.

Trains were constantly improved. By 1920 the trains were much larger, faster, and more comfortable than the first ones.

The streamlined trains of today are even better. Their powerful engines and beautiful cars make modern travel safe and pleasant.

As the country learned better ways of traveling, it learned better ways of living. The railroads carried people and goods from one place to another. The people in all parts of the country seemed closer together. They exchanged goods. They shared ideas. They all worked together to improve our country still more.

Boats and ships also helped the people to improve our ways of living. Many of the pioneers carried their goods down the rivers on flatboats and keelboats. The flatboats were like large rafts with little cabins built in the center. The flatboats usually floated down the rivers, but occasionally they were rowed with oars.

The keelboats were longer than the flatboats and not so wide. They had oars and sometimes a sail. Often they were "poled." When the boat was poled, it was guided near the edge of the stream. Then the men put their poles into the river bed. They pushed on the poles and walked from the front of the boat to the back. Then they picked up their poles, walked to the front of the boat, and poled again. This moved the boat forward.

Occasionally the boat was pulled by a horse. The horse walked very slowly along the bank of the river and pulled on a heavy rope that was fastened to the boat.

Along the Mississippi the pioneers shipped their produce to market on the flatboats. The farmers who lived inland were not so fortunate. It cost them a great deal of money to ship their produce by wagon or by train. Soon people began to talk of building canals, or making waterways, to connect the rivers. Then they could travel many places upon the swift-flowing rivers.

One of the first canals to be built was the *Erie Canal.* When engineers talked of building it, people laughed at them. "You cannot build a canal over three hundred miles long. You cannot build it where the great forests of New York State now stand," they said.

But men *did* build the canal. They worked hard for eight long years. They cut down the trees of the forest. They moved tons of earth to build the "big ditch." When it was finished, the people fired cannons and made speeches. The canal connected Lake Erie with the Hudson River. It opened up a waterway far to the west!

ROBERT FULTON'S STEAMBOAT

A large crowd of people gathered along the Hudson River. Some of them came because they were curious. Others came to scoff and to laugh. A boat was tied at the river dock. On the side of the boat was a large paddle wheel. The paddle wheel moved slightly with the rippling waters.

The people looked at the boat curiously. "It is Robert Fulton's *steamboat,*" said one man. "But it will fail. Steam cannot run a boat as large as that!"

"Fulton has been told to keep it off the river unless it will travel *four miles an hour,*" said another man. Then he shook his head. "Fulton is dreaming great dreams," he said, "but they will not come true."

A cloud of black smoke poured from the chimney near the center of the boat. The engine gave a chugging sound as it started. Then the paddle wheel on the side of the boat began to turn. *Would it move the boat?*

The people watched eagerly. In a few moments the wheel began to turn faster. It churned the waters of the river into a splashing white foam. Then the boat began to move, slowly at first, then a little faster. A cheer went up from the people along the riverbank. Boats *could* be run by steam! Fulton's invention was successful!

Robert Fulton's steamboat was very crude. It traveled only five miles an hour. But it proved to the people that boats could be run by steam.

FASTER SAILING SHIPS

Robert Fulton invented his steamboat even before the Erie Canal was dug. But for a time men still used many sailing ships. American shipbuilders made a fast sailing ship called a *packet.*

The packets were sturdy ships. They sailed between certain ports just as ocean liners do today. They carried both freight and passengers from the Old World to the New, and around the tip of South America to the West Coast.

Then *clipper ships* were made. The clipper ships were very much like the packet ships, only larger. They had many white sails that billowed in the wind. They were larger and had more sails than any other sailing vessel that was ever made. During the gold rush in California, clipper ships sailed around South America and up the West Coast. They carried many "forty-niners" from the East Coast to San Francisco. They carried mail and supplies to the men who were working in the gold fields.

The clipper ships were built in the shipyards along the coast of Maine. They were fast sailing ships and for a number of years people were not interested in building steamships that would travel upon the ocean.

But as time went on, the people began to think more and more about Fulton's steamboat. They knew that other steamboats had been built and were in use upon the lakes and rivers. *Could a steamship be made that would travel upon the ocean?*

The first steamships were not successful. But men soon learned how to improve them. Today modern steamships plow swiftly through the ocean waters. They travel much faster than the old clipper ships and are safer and far more comfortable.

The steamships of today are like little floating cities. They have swimming pools, beautiful lounging rooms, libraries, motion-picture shows, tennis courts, beauty parlors, and barbershops. They have everything to make a journey upon the ocean pleasant and comfortable.

The canals and waterways, the railroads, the steamboats, and the sailing vessels helped to bring the people of the nation closer together. The modern steamships have brought the nations of the world closer together. All these things have helped to improve our ways of living.

The pioneers shipped their goods down the rivers on flatboats and keelboats. The boats usually floated with the river current.

Boats were sometimes pulled by horses. A horse walked along the riverbank, pulling on a rope fastened to the boat.

It was easier to travel by water than by land. Canals were built to join the rivers. The Erie Canal was one of the first to be opened.

Robert Fulton invented a steamboat to travel on rivers. People were surprised that it would run five miles an hour.

Sailing ships were used for ocean travel. The Clipper ships, with their many big sails, were the fastest sailing ships of that time.

Steamships for ocean travel were also built. Modern liners are like little floating cities. They travel to every port in the world.

For hundreds of years men wondered how birds could soar through the air so easily and so gracefully. For hundreds of years they wondered why people could not fly, too. Even in ancient times, the Greeks and the Romans were so eager to fly that they made statues of horses and men with wings.

They also wrote stories that told about men's flying. An ancient Greek inventor was supposed to have made a wooden bird that would fly. The story, or legend, says the bird flew about fifty feet.

No one really knows whether the people in olden times ever tried to fly. But while the colonies were being settled, a Frenchman made a successful gliding flight. By using cloth wings that opened and shut like a book, he glided from a high window to the ground. This flight led to other experiments in flying.

While our country was growing larger, many men were experimenting with balloons and gliders. One man in England even built a model of a steam-driven airplane. But the most successful of the early inventors was a German engineer named Otto Lilienthal. Lilienthal made several gliders and kept a careful record of his experiments. He was the first man to stay aloft in a "flying machine."

But none of the early attempts to fly was really successful. The men who are called "the pioneers of flying" were *Orville* and *Wilbur Wright.*

The Wright brothers owned a bicycle repair shop in Dayton, Ohio, but they studied gliding as a hobby. They read Lilienthal's book. They watched the birds in flight. They examined pictures of gliders and tried to learn from the mistakes of other inventors.

304

After studying for four years, they made a glider. They decided to test their glider at Kitty Hawk, North Carolina. They chose Kitty Hawk because the wind from the ocean blew steadily at eighteen miles an hour, and the high sand dunes would serve as runways for the take-off. To their delight the glider worked!

In the next few years they built larger and better gliders. Then they decided to build a "flying machine" with a gasoline engine. When the plane was finished, the Wrights shipped it to Kitty Hawk, too. They invited the people in the town to come and watch them test it. Only five men and one boy came out to watch the flight!

On December 17, 1903, Orville Wright climbed into the plane and started the engine. The plane rolled down a little track. Then it began to lift from the ground and rise into the air. Would it really fly? *It stayed in the air for twelve seconds!*

The Wright brothers were overjoyed. They tried three more flights. On the fourth flight the plane stayed in the air fifty-nine seconds and flew eight hundred fifty-two feet. This flight marked the beginning of the air age!

Later the Wright brothers improved their plane. Other people built planes, too. Year after year better planes were built. Today fast planes fly to all parts of the world. They have made neighbors of all the countries of the world.

The first successful glider in the United States was built by the Wrights. They tried it out at Kitty Hawk, North Carolina.

Then they decided to build a "flying machine" with a gasoline engine. The airplane surprised everyone by flying twelve seconds.

After planes were improved Charles Lindbergh flew alone across the Atlantic. His plane was the *Spirit of St. Louis*.

Later, Admiral Byrd flew a plane over the South Pole. With airplanes men could go places they had only dreamed of going.

The helicopter, too, has many uses. It carries mail. It picks up soldiers wounded in battle. It can land where a plane cannot.

The airplane of today is fast and safe. It can fly quickly across the continent. It can cross the oceans to foreign lands.

There was no mail service in the early colonies. Occasionally a rich man sent letters by special messenger. But the poor people could not send letters at all.

As the colonies grew larger, the colonial governments hired men to carry the mail. Some of the colonial mailmen walked; others rode horses. A few even skated on the ice in the wintertime. Mail was delivered from house to house, from town to town, and from colony to colony. When the mail was sent some distance, it was carried by men on horseback or by stagecoach.

As the pioneers moved westward, mail service moved west, too. In 1858 the government established the *overland mail service*. Light wagons were first used to carry both mail and passengers. Then stagecoaches were used.

Along the overland road were *home stations* and *swing stations*. At the home stations, drivers were changed and meals were served. At the swing stations, the tired horses were changed for fresh ones.

Day and night the coaches rumbled over the rocky, dusty roads as fast as the horses could travel. They went through floods and storms! Often they were attacked by Indians! *But they carried the mail.*

Then came a faster mail service to the West. Before railroads were built across America, the *pony express* was organized. Men riding swift ponies carried the mail between Missouri and California. The ponies were fast, the riders light. Stations were built every ten or fifteen miles along the way. The stations were usually built near a spring or a water hole. The rider rode from one station to another as fast as his pony could travel. Then he changed ponies and was on his way again.

The letters were written on very thin paper. Then they were wrapped in oiled silk to keep them from becoming soiled or wet. The mail was carried in leather bags fastened to a leather square. When the square was thrown over the saddle, the bags rested on each side of the horse.

Each rider rode from seventy-five to one hundred miles a day. He was allowed just two minutes to change horses at each stop. When the weather was good it took about ten days to carry a letter from St. Louis to San Francisco. Today air mail can go twice as far in one day!

THE TELEGRAPH IS INVENTED

While the pioneers were traveling to the West, inventors were trying to find a way to send messages through the air by electricity. As they worked, they learned many things about electricity. But they did not discover how to send messages.

Samuel F. B. Morse made a good living as a portrait painter. But one day he heard men talking about electricity. He became interested and began to learn all he could about the way electricity works.

After he had studied for some time he thought to himself, "An electric wire will act as a magnet. I wonder if I can make the magnet strike hard enough to make marks

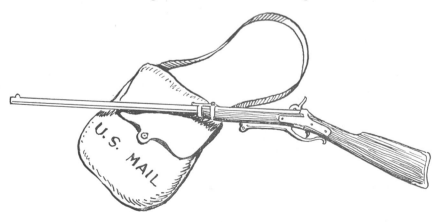

upon a tape. If I can, perhaps I can find a way to send messages by electricity."

Morse worked for many hours. He found a way to make the electricity tap out short and long dashes, or "dots and dashes." Then he arranged the dots and dashes to represent each letter of the alphabet. Now came another problem. Could he send messages long distances?

He taught his assistant how to read the dots and dashes, or the *Morse Code*. Then he wound three miles of wire around his house. He put a receiving set in one room and a sending set in another room.

His assistant stood by the receiving set. Morse went into the room where the sending set was placed. He made the electricity spell out the words, "A patient waiter is no loser." His assistant received and read the message correctly. The *telegraph* worked!

Morse showed his telegraph at a public meeting. A man named Alfred Vail became interested and decided to join Morse. Morse did not have enough money to build a line to see if the telegraph would work for a still greater distance. But Congress voted the money to build a line between Washington and Baltimore.

On May 24, 1844, the test was made. Morse was in Washington. Vail was in Baltimore. Morse flashed over the wires the message, "What hath God wrought!" Vail received the message in Baltimore and flashed it back. The telegraph was a success!

Telegraph wires were put up all over the country and messages were flashed back and forth. Then Cyrus W. Field dreamed of sending messages to Europe. For ten years he tried to lay a heavy wire, or cable, under the Atlantic Ocean. Finally he succeeded. The people in America could now send cablegrams to the people in Europe!

Then a cable was laid across the Pacific Ocean. Today nearly every country in the world has an ocean cable that connects it with the rest of the world.

As time went on, the telegraph was improved. A man named Marconi learned to send electric messages without wires. The *wireless telegraph* is now used in all parts of the world. The *wireless telephone* is also used. Modern *radio* and *television* have found a place in many homes.

All these things have brought the people of the United States and of the world closer together. They have made our way of life more pleasant.

BELL INVENTS THE TELEPHONE

Alexander Graham Bell was a speech teacher in Boston. He tried to teach the deaf to talk. While he was teaching, he became interested in inventions. He wanted to invent something that would improve the telegraph.

He learned many things about sending sound over wires. He wondered if voices could be sent over wires, too. He experimented for a long time. Finally he believed that he had found the answer.

He and a friend, Thomas A. Watson, began to work on Bell's plans for a "talking machine." They made a number of instruments. None of them worked!

The men were often discouraged, but they did not give up. One day Watson heard Bell's voice over the wire. "Mr. Watson, please come here. I want you." The men were filled with joy. Voices *could* be sent over the wires!

The telephone, one of the greatest wonders of the world, had been invented. But many improvements have been added to that first simple telephone. Today we can talk to people in any part of the world.

At first the colonists had no way to send mail. Later the governments hired men to carry the mail. Some walked—others rode.

The stagecoach carried mail from one town to another. It took six weeks for a letter to go from Virginia to New York.

In the West, part of the mail was carried by Pony Express. This express was the fastest mail service known at that time.

Improvement in communication was soon made. Samuel Morse invented the telegraph. It would send messages by electricity.

Then Alexander Graham Bell invented the telephone. It was a joyful moment when Bell and Watson knew that the telephone would work!

Today telephone and telegraph lines extend to all parts of the world. Radio and television, too, are used by people in many lands.

THINGS TO DO

1. Make a series of cartoons that will show how roads in the United States were improved.

2. Collect pictures of old wagons, carriages, and stagecoaches that were used by the colonists and the pioneers. Make a chart for your classroom.

3. Write a short paragraph explaining why you think better ways of traveling helped the nation to progress.

4. Write a humorous poem about a ride on one of the early trains in America.

5. Choose sides and play the game of charades. Let one side act out some scene from the story you have just read. Let the other side guess what scene is being acted. Let each side have a chance to act and to guess. There are many things you might act out, such as the invention of the telephone, the invention of the telegraph, and the story of the first airplane flight of the Wright brothers at Kitty Hawk.

6. Pretend that you were a rider on the pony express. Write a short story telling about what you did in one day. Tell what you saw as your horse galloped from station to station.

LET'S TALK ABOUT—

1. How better roads and better ways of traveling helped the nation to progress.

2. How the Americans of yesterday helped you to enjoy the things you have today.

3. How and why our ways of living have changed.

4. How better ways of traveling and sending messages have brought the people of the world closer together.

NEW WORDS

If you do not know the following words, look them up. Talk about the words in class. Add to your word file any words you did not know.

manufactured	cultivator	immigrants
warehouses	chaff	restaurant
sickle	operator	

NAMES YOU WILL MEET IN THE NEXT STORY

Samuel Slater	Elias Howe	Eli Whitney
Cyrus McCormick		Thomas A. Edison

In the story of our country many things were happening at the same time. New lands were being added to make our country still larger. Pioneers were building homes farther and farther west. Men were learning new and better ways of traveling and of sending messages.

They were also learning many other things. Some of the things changed our ways of living still more.

After you have read this story, talk about how the Machine Age came to America. Talk about how it brought many changes. Talk about how the changes helped to make the United States a good place to live.

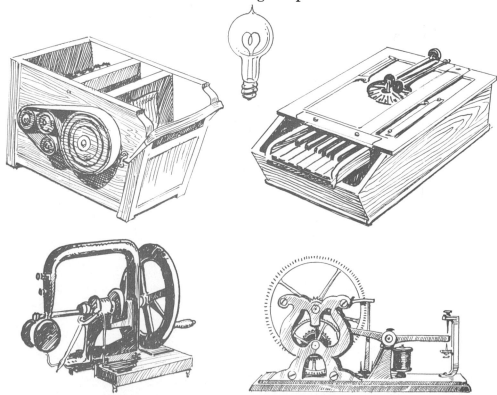

NEW MACHINES
AND MORE CHANGES

FACTORIES ARE BUILT

When America was young, there were no factories here. There were no machines to help the people with their work. In the fields and in the home the work was all done by hand. The hand labor was slow and tiresome!

In England, the *spinning jenny* and the *power loom*, machines to spin and to weave thread, had been invented. At first the machines were turned by hand. Then they were run by water power. After James Watt invented the steam engine, the machines were run by steam.

The later colonists shipped rice, cotton, tobacco, wool, and other products to England. In return, they bought goods made in the English factories. England made a great deal of money by selling her manufactured goods to the Americans. She did not want the colonists to learn to make the machines that were used in the English factories. To prevent this, laws were passed that would not allow anyone to take the machines or the plans for building them out of the country.

A young Englishman named Samuel Slater came to America. He had worked in the English factories and could remember the whirring machines and the big power looms. With only his memory to guide him, he began to build a machine. He built the first successful spinning machine in America that was run by water power.

317

After the invention of the spinning machine, many factories for spinning cotton thread were begun in the North. The factories needed more and more cotton. The cotton came from the large plantations in the South. But the cotton growers were having difficulty.

A ripe boll of cotton looks soft and fluffy. But inside the fluffy boll are hard seeds. The seeds cling tightly to the cotton fibers that are used for spinning.

It took a good worker nearly a day to pick the seeds from one pound of cotton! The southern planters knew they could not send enough cotton to the northern factories unless they could find a better way to clean the cotton. "The people in the North have machines to help them spin the thread. We must have a machine to help us pick the seeds from the cotton," they said.

Not long after Samuel Slater built his spinning machine, a young man named Eli Whitney went to Georgia to visit a friend of his. While there, he heard some of the Georgia planters talk about cleaning the cotton. Whitney became interested in the problem.

In a short while he built a simple box-like machine with rows of wire teeth inside. When the crank on the outside of the box was turned, the cotton passed through the machine and the wire teeth pulled out the cotton seeds.

With this machine, or cotton "gin," one man could clean as much cotton as ten men could clean by hand. *If the machine could be run by water power, it would clean as much as fifty men could clean by hand!*

After the cotton gin was invented, great fields of cotton were planted in the South. Soon the planters were growing more cotton than the northern factories could use.

The northern mills were spinning the cotton thread, but the cotton cloth was still woven by hand. Power looms like those in England were needed. *But again there were no plans.* Again men had to build the machines from memory! By 1814, a mill in Massachusetts was weaving a very good cotton cloth.

Not long after this, other power looms were made and other factories were built. Work that had taken hours to do by hand was now done in a few minutes in the factories. The *Machine Age* in America was beginning.

The first factories were gloomy and dark. They were often built in large barns or in empty warehouses. Women and girls operated the new machines. Often they worked as long as fifteen hours a day and received only two dollars a week for their work.

But as the years went by, both factories and machines were improved. The factories were built of brick, concrete, and steel. They were built with many windows in them, so they would be both light and airy. The factory workers were paid much better. They worked shorter hours. New machines were invented—machines for doing many kinds of work that had been done by hand.

Today nearly everything used in American homes, in the schools, on the farms, and in business offices is made in a factory. The machines and factories have given us many things the early Americans did not have!

In early colonial days all spinning and weaving were done by hand. It was hard to make enough cloth for all the family's clothing.

Then a man named Samuel Slater made a spinning machine. Another inventor built a power loom. Cloth was made in factories.

The factories in New England needed cotton. But growers in the South could not produce as much as was needed in the busy mills.

The South had plenty of cotton, but it took a long time to pick out the seeds by hand. A good worker could clean a pound a day.

Then Eli Whitney made the cotton gin. The gin was turned with a crank and cleaned as much as ten men could clean by hand.

A power gin could clean as much cotton as fifty men could clean. There was now enough cotton for the Northern mills.

Not so long ago the farmers in the United States did most of their work by hand. They walked up and down the fields sowing the seed by hand. They used hoes for weeding and for loosening the ground around the growing crops. They used oxen or horses to draw their crude plows. They threshed the grain with heavy flails.

The first colonists cut their grain with a sickle. But it was a long, tiresome task. Then a tool called the *cradle* was invented. The cradle had a sharp blade for cutting the grain and a frame to catch the stalks after they were cut. The cradle was much better than the sickle, but it was still hard work to cut the grain.

As the pioneers moved west, their farms were larger. They wanted better farming tools. Machines for sowing wheat and planting corn were made. The plow was improved. Then men began to think about a machine to cut the grain.

A number of men made such a machine, but the best *reaper* was invented by Cyrus McCormick. For some time McCormick had been interested in making a machine to cut grain. "It takes a long time to cut grain with a cradle," he said. "I will make a machine that will cut the grain faster and with less work. I will make a reaper that can be drawn by horses, so the men can ride."

McCormick invented a reaper that was pulled by a horse. The reaper had long knives that cut the ripened grain. In the center of the reaper there was a little platform where the grain was thrown after it was cut.

When McCormick was ready to test his reaper, he drove it into a field. Nearly a hundred people were there to watch him. Most of them were unfriendly. Most of them made fun of the crude machine.

As McCormick began the test his heart sank. The field was rough and uneven. The reaper jerked up and down and rocked from side to side. The wheat was not cut smoothly.

The people began to laugh. The man who owned the field rushed up and ordered McCormick to stop. Then another farmer stepped forward. "I own a field across the way," he said. "You may continue the test in my field."

McCormick took the reaper to the field across the road. This field was smooth and level. The reaper cut the grain in wide, even patches. At the end of the day six acres of grain had been cut. The crowd no longer laughed. The people knew that the reaper would work.

Other men began to invent farm machinery, too. They made plows with sharp steel blades, cultivators to break up the soil, and seeders to sow the grain. They invented a thresher that would separate the grain from the chaff.

But the farmers were still not satisfied. They wanted even better ways of working. The inventors made new machines that were much better than the old ones. They made larger plows with several steel blades. They made larger cultivators that would weed several rows of plants at one time. They improved the seeders.

A new machine was invented to replace the old reaper. It was a machine that cut the grain and threshed it at the same time. This machine is called a *combine*. It is one of the most useful machines the farmer has ever used.

Then the gasoline tractor was invented. The tractor pulled the heavy machines faster than horses could pull them. Not all of the farmers own the new machines. Many of them still have small farms. Many are still using machines pulled by horses. But the farming methods of today are quite different from the methods used by the early colonists and the western pioneers.

Farming was hard work for the colonists. They used very crude plows, sowed seed by hand, and cut grain with a long sickle.

Then a cradle was invented. The cradle had a sharp blade for cutting the grain and a frame to catch the stalks after they were cut.

The cradle was better than the sickle, but the farmer still had to thresh his grain by hitting it with heavy flails to separate the grain from the chaff.

The reaper McCormick invented helped the farmer a great deal. It could cut grain faster and with less work.

The combine is another machine that helps the farmer. It cuts and threshes the grain, and sacks it, ready for market.

Modern plows turn several furrows at one time. Cultivators weed many rows. Seeders plant crops. Tractors pull the machinery.

THE INVENTION OF
THE SEWING MACHINE

Cloth was woven in the busy northern factories. But for a long time women still continued to sew by hand. One night, about a hundred years ago, a man named Elias Howe sat watching his wife as she stitched a garment.

"What a long time it takes to sew by hand," he thought. "I wonder if a sewing *machine* could be made."

Howe worked on his idea for a long time. He watched the machines in the mills. He remembered how his wife's needle went through the cloth as she sewed.

By 1846 he had made a machine that sewed. But the women would not buy it. They did not believe that a machine could stitch as well as they could sew by hand.

For a while Howe had a very difficult time. Then a few women started to use the sewing machines. They liked them. Other women began to use them. Little by little the sewing machine found a place in American homes.

326

"You must work, work, work, and then work some more."
This is what Thomas A. Edison said when someone asked
him how to be successful. He believed in his own advice.
His whole life was spent in hard work.

Out of his hard work came many inventions. He invented
so many things he has often been called the "wizard" of
America. He helped to improve the telephone, the telegraph,
the typewriter, and motion pictures.

Shortly after the telephone was invented, Edison invented
a machine that would *record* sounds and *repeat* them. He
called the machine the phonograph.

The story of how he invented the phonograph is very interesting. Edison worked for some time as a telegraph oper-
ator. Many times there were not enough operators to take
all the messages that came over the wires.

Edison thought about the problem. "I would like to invent a machine that would record messages," he said. "I
would like to make the machine repeat the messages."

Edison drew the plans for such a machine. He gave the
plans to one of his assistants and told him to build the
machine. When the machine was finished, Edison recited
into it "Mary Had a Little Lamb." He repeated the words
slowly and clearly. Then he turned a crank on the machine. His own words came back to him! The phonograph
had been invented!

People listened in wonder when they heard of the new
machine. From all over the world Edison received letters
and telegrams of praise. He had made one of his most
famous discoveries.

Thomas A. Edison was one of the greatest inventors of
all time. During his life he patented more than one

thousand inventions. He helped to change the ways
of living in America and in the whole world.

Much of Edison's work had to do with lighting and
electricity. A large street lamp had already been made.
Edison wanted to make a small light that could be used
in homes. He worked night and day trying to invent such
a light. He did not want to take time to eat. He slept
only a few hours each night.

Finally he learned how to make a fine carbon wire that
would not burn up under strong heat. He found a way to
pump the air out of a glass bulb, put in the carbon wire,
and then seal the bulb. This was the first successful light
bulb.

From this light bulb came all of our modern lighting.
Homes, factories, churches, schools, highways, and city

streets are lighted by Edison's great invention. He truly made electricity the servant of man.

When he died in 1931 he was eighty-four years old. Just a few weeks before his death he said to his friends, "I shall not stop working until I am one hundred. I have many things I want to do."

Edison wanted his inventions to help people. His dream of helping the world came true. It is often said of him, "He was the world's most useful citizen."

MACHINES CHANGE OUR WAYS OF LIVING

The inventions of machines changed our ways of living. Our homes are much better than the homes of the early Americans. Our clothes and our foods are better, too.

The *Machine Age* has given us many things. Lumber, brick, glass, metal, cement, and other materials used in homes are made with machinery. Modern inventions cool our homes in the summer and heat them in the winter. Most of our houses have running water in the kitchen and in the bathroom. Nearly all of them are wired for electricity. It would be difficult to imagine a house built without the aid of machinery!

The invention of machinery has helped us to have better clothes. Much of the work of spinning, weaving, cutting, and sewing is now done in factories. Most of the clothes are better and cheaper than those made by hand.

Machines have given us many new foods. Today most of the foods in grocery stores are prepared in factories. The American people no longer eat only the foods they raise. Foods are shipped to us from all parts of the world.

The Machine Age has truly given us more *foods*, better *clothes*, and better *homes!*

Early Americans pumped water at the town pump and took it home in wooden pails or buckets. A few had pumps in their yards.

The women did their washing by hand. They rubbed clothes on a washboard, boiled the white ones, and hung them out to dry.

They roasted meat on a spit, cooked food over the open fire, and did their baking in a stone oven at the side of the big fireplace.

Americans no longer have to get their water at a town pump. Water is now piped into the home, ready for use when needed.

Washing now is much easier than in colonial days. Our modern washers, dryers, and ironers all help the busy housewife.

Cooking is also much easier today. Modern refrigerators keep the food fresh. Gas and electric stoves cook the food evenly as well as quickly.

Today there are many small towns and villages in the United States. There are also large cities. The cities have grown because of the Machine Age, or *the invention of many kinds of machinery*.

When America was young, the people lived on farms scattered throughout the country. They raised their own food, built their own homes, and made their own clothes. Then machines were invented and factories were built.

The busy mills and factories needed workers to operate the machinery. Men, and a few women, moved from the farms to the little towns where the factories were built. But many of them were not happy in the mills. When land on the frontier became easy to obtain, they decided to go west to earn their living.

At first the mill owners were disappointed when the workers moved west. But it was not long until people from Europe took their places. The *immigrants* who came from the Old World found America a good place to live, and they were happy working in the factories.

Most of the early mills were textile mills, or *mills for spinning and weaving cloth*. Later, there were other factories that made machinery, tools, clocks, brick, glass, paper, shoes, furniture, and many other things.

The new factories were larger than the early mills. As the factories became larger, more and more workers were needed. Soon the factory towns were no longer towns, or villages. They were thriving cities.

The growth of large cities changed our ways of living. People no longer did many different kinds of work. Men and women began to do just *one* kind of work. They depended upon other people for many of the things they needed.

During colonial days there were no police departments. The men took turns watching at night. In a large city this would not be possible. As the cities grew larger, police departments were organized. Today, policemen protect the *people*, their *homes*, and their *property* at all times of the day and night.

In early America, the only fire department was a "bucket brigade." Whenever there was a fire, men and boys, carrying large buckets, came running from all parts of town.

They formed a line from the fire to the nearest well or stream of water. The buckets were filled with water and passed rapidly from one person to another. When the bucket reached the end of the line, the water was thrown onto the fire. Sometimes the fire was put out, but more often the house burned to the ground.

Today all cities have fire departments and well-trained firemen. The firemen are paid wages. They are taught how to fight fires, how to rescue persons from burning buildings, and how to administer first aid.

Cities also do many other things for the people. All cities provide pure fresh water for the people to use. They employ men to inspect the food that is sold in stores. They have men to inspect dairy farms, restaurants, and bakeries. They build public hospitals, libraries, parks, swimming pools, and public playgrounds.

Cities remove trash and garbage, and clean the streets. They build and repair bridges, streets, underpasses, and overpasses. They light the city streets and mark them with names and numbers.

The early Americans took care of themselves and their own needs. The people in a city *work together* to make life safer and more pleasant for all. *The Machine Age has brought many, many changes!*

In colonial days the little towns had no policemen. The men took turns watching at night. Often the watchman called the time.

Fighting fires was difficult. The "bucket brigades" tried to put out the fires, but too often the house or building burned to the ground.

Farmers often went from door to door selling fruits and vegetables. The only way to have fruit in winter was to preserve it.

With the Machine Age came modern cities. Each city has a police department. Police guard the city and the people at all times.

Modern firemen learn how to fight fires in the best and quickest way. Their equipment reaches the tallest skyscrapers.

The Machine Age gave us many foods. Today we can go into a market and buy fresh foods, canned foods, and frozen foods.

THINGS TO DO

1. Let the class make a list of the things pupils have used today. Talk about those that were made with the help of machines and those that were made by hand. Were most of the things on your list made with machines?

2. If you live near a factory, arrange to visit it. When you come back, talk about how the machines in the factory helped the workers. Talk about how they help you.

3. Collect pictures of modern farm machinery. Draw pictures of early farm machinery. Make charts of your pictures.

4. Read more about the life of Thomas A. Edison. Tell the class some of the most interesting things you read. Write a short paragraph telling why Edison has been called "The World's Most Useful Citizen."

5. Make a list of the food you ate yesterday. In what ways did the Machine Age help you to enjoy them?

6. Take two sheets of paper. On one sheet make a heading "The Things in My Home That Were Made with Machinery." On the other sheet make the heading "The Things in My Home That Were Made without the Help of Machines."

   List some of the things you have in your home under one of the two headings. Remember that if your mother sewed something by hand she used needles and thread that were made in a factory.

LET'S TALK ABOUT—

1. How the desire to improve our ways of living brought new inventions and new changes.

2. How a factory of today compares with one of the first factories in the United States.

3. How the *Machine Age* helped our country.
4. How inventions changed our ways of living.
5. How your city government helps *you.*

NEW WORDS

The following words are used in the next story. Some of them may be new to you. Look up any you do not know. Then talk about them in class. Put in your word file the words you did not know.

circuit	democratic	conserve
baptized	pursuit	resource
performed	dictator	

NAMES YOU WILL MEET IN THE NEXT STORY

Horace Mann	Pearl Harbor	Woodrow Wilson
Hitler	General Assembly	Korea
Security Council		Communists

Before You Read the Story —

The Americans of yesterday gave you a rich heritage. The colonists, the pioneers, the inventors, and the workers all helped to make our country as it is today. It is a good country. It is one of the best countries in the world. Each year it is becoming an even better place in which to live.

Now it is up to *you*. You are still boys and girls, but you must keep America a good place to live. When you are grown, you must make it a *better* place.

After you have read this story, talk about why the United States is a good country. Talk about how *you* can help to make it an even better place to live.

AMERICA—
A GOOD PLACE TO LIVE

"... that government of the people, by the people, for the people, shall not perish from the earth." As President Lincoln spoke these words, a hush fell over the men and women gathered at Gettysburg. They knew that the words were more than a part of a prepared speech—they were a prayer in the heart of the man who said them.

President Lincoln believed in his country and he believed in the people. He wanted the Union to be united and to serve the needs of the people. He wanted the people to be free to *work together* and to build this country into a happy and prosperous nation.

Many men knew that Lincoln's speech at Gettysburg would long be remembered. They did not know that the words "of the people, by the people, for the people" would become an ideal of good government. They did not know that the words would help to pattern our way of life.

The government of the United States is a republic, or a democracy. A democracy is a government "of the people," organized by the people, and controlled by the people. It is not run for the benefit of one man or a small group of men. It is run for the benefit of all.

Under our democratic government, the American people have gradually developed a better way of life. They have been free to do many, many things that make our country a good place in which to live.

339

FREE EDUCATION FOR ALL

There are many things that make a country a good place to live. The right to go to good schools is one of them. In colonial and pioneer times most of the people believed that only the children of the rich should have an education. "There is no need for poor boys to go to school," they said. "They should do the work."

But one man did not believe this! *Horace Mann* was a poor boy who lived on a little farm in Massachusetts. When he did not work on the farm, he worked in a factory to earn money. Occasionally he went to school. He wanted an education but the schools offered little opportunity. The teachers spent most of their time punishing the boys instead of teaching them.

"The United States will never become a great nation unless its people can read and write," thought Horace Mann. "I would like to see public schools for everyone—the poor and the rich alike."

When Horace Mann was grown he became a lawyer and won high positions in his state. But he kept thinking about the idea of free education for all. Finally he gave up his law practice and spent most of his time working for free schools.

For a long time the people would not listen to him. Then a few people began to believe in his idea. Then more and more people began to think that he was right. "American boys and girls should have an opportunity to go to good schools," the people began to say to one another.

Little by little the idea of free education spread to all parts of the nation. More and more free schools were built. The idea Horace Mann was willing to devote his life to was the beginning of our schools of today.

CHURCHES IN AMERICA

Churches also make a country a good place in which to live. You have read about the early colonial churches. The pioneer churches were quite different. Most of the frontier villages had a church, but very few of them could afford a preacher.

One preacher rode around to many small towns. He visited each town once or twice a year. The circle of towns he visited was called a circuit. In each town he held church services and baptized new members.

When a circuit preacher visited a town, people for miles around came to hear him. They stayed for several days. Some of them slept in wagons. Others brought tents to sleep in. The meetings were called *camp meetings*. At the camp meetings many men, women, and children joined the church. There was always great excitement over the preaching, the singing, and the baptizing of new members.

As the towns grew larger, more and more of them could afford a preacher. Today there are few towns in the United States without a full-time minister. The minister spends much of his time working for the religious welfare of the people.

Many Americans prefer to live in a town where the influence of the church is strong. The churches help people to live better lives. They teach them to be honest and truthful—to be loyal to their God and to their country.

In colonial times, only the rich went to school. A man named Horace Mann devoted his life to obtaining free schools for all.

Most frontier towns had one church. But usually the only minister was a circuit preacher who came to town once or twice a year.

Today, modern buildings, attractive playgrounds, and good transportation make going to school easier and more pleasant.

Now nearly every town in the United States has one or more churches. Almost every church has its own minister.

LIFE, LIBERTY, AND THE PURSUIT OF HAPPINESS

When the colonists signed the Declaration of Independence, they began the fight for freedom in America. Since that time many changes have taken place, but the American people of today still believe as the colonists believed— that all men should have the right to guide their lives in their own way.

There is one part of the Declaration that says that all men have the right to "life, liberty, and the pursuit of happiness." The *protection of life*, the *right to liberty*, and the *right to seek happiness* are the ideals upon which our government was founded. They are rights that are guaranteed to every man, woman, and child in the United States.

In some countries of the world the people do not have these rights. Their government is controlled by a small group of men who care little about the rights of the people. Perhaps a true story may help you to understand what can happen when people are not free.

●

In a little town in Europe lived a humble peasant. He, his wife, and his four children had worked hard. Their few acres of wheat were well tended. Their cattle and their hogs were fat. Their house, though small, was neat and cheerful.

The peasant and his family were a little better off than their neighbors. They had worked harder and saved more. They were kindly people, ready to help a neighbor in need. They harmed no one; they expected no one to harm them.

But their dictator did not care about the needs of his people. One day the agents of the dictator came and seized the peasant's crops. They took his cattle and his fat hogs. They took away the barrels of rosy-cheeked apples that he had stored in his barn.

They took away his golden pumpkins, his potatoes, his cabbages, and his wheat. They did not even pay for them. They left the peasant and his family to starve!

●

This happened not so long ago in a country in Europe. It cannot happen in the United States. In the United States all of the people have the right to "life, liberty, and the pursuit of happiness."

There are many, many ways in which our *lives* are protected. Every day firemen in all parts of the country protect our lives and our property. Each day the police departments protect people from injury and death.

Public health departments also protect our lives. They carry on war against all kinds of diseases that cripple and kill. They inspect meat and dairy products to see that these foods are wholesome and fit for use. They try in every way possible to protect the life and health of everyone.

Liberty is another important right of the American people. In the United States the people are free to say what they think, read what they choose, go to the church they like, and choose the kind of work they wish to do. They are free to choose their own leaders and to help make their own laws.

The right to the *pursuit of happiness* is also a privilege of the American people. So long as a person does not hurt someone else, *so long as he does not break any laws*, he is free to do the things that will bring him the most happiness.

The ragged colonial armies fought for the rights of "life, liberty, and the pursuit of happiness." It seems strange that many years later American soldiers again had to fight for these same rights!

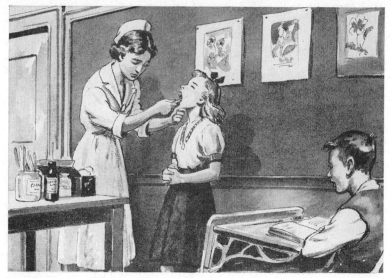

In our country we believe everyone has a right to "life, liberty, and the pursuit of happiness." Even in school "life" is protected.

Boys and girls have "liberty" to choose their friends, the clubs or organizations they wish to belong to, and the work they wish to do.

The right to choose their own hobbies is one of their privileges. It is part of the right to the "pursuit of happiness."

346

Adult workers are constantly searching for new ways to protect the life and the health of every person in the United States.

The liberty of each person in our country is protected by the courts. If a man feels he is treated unfairly he may ask for justice.

Americans seek happiness in many different ways. The right to travel wherever one pleases brings happiness to many people.

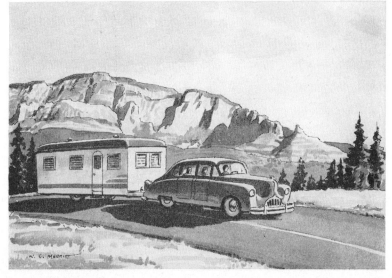

In 1914 war broke out in Europe—a war that was to be called World War I. Germany and Austria were on one side. England, France, Russia, and Italy were on the other. Most of the smaller countries of Europe also declared war and joined one side or the other.

For a time we sold war supplies to both sides, but this led to trouble. The English Navy blockaded our ships that were being sent to Germany. German submarines sank the ships we were sending to England. The German submarines also sank ships on which Americans were traveling. Many American citizens were drowned.

President Woodrow Wilson sent a note of warning to Germany. He told her that she must stop sinking our ships and killing our citizens. Germany answered by threatening to sink any American ship that entered certain waters.

The United States could no longer keep out of war! On April 6, 1917, we joined the First World War on the side of France and England.

A little over a year after we entered the war, the Germans surrendered. *They surrendered on November 11, 1918.* This is the date we celebrate as Armistice Day— the day the fighting stopped in World War I.

A SECOND WORLD WAR

When we entered World War I, President Wilson told the other nations that we did not want new territory. We wanted only to help make the world "safe for democracy." We believed we had done so.

But as the years passed, *dictators* came into power in some nations. The dictators ruled in a cruel and unjust manner. They took away many of the rights and privileges of the people. They controlled the newspapers and the radios. They punished, and sometimes put to death, anyone who disagreed with them. The people were no longer free. They were servants of the dictator, and of the State.

For a time the dictators were satisfied to rule only their own people. Then they wanted to rule other countries as well. Hitler, the dictator in Germany, sent his soldiers into some of the smaller countries of Europe. The German soldiers marched across northern Europe, conquering one small nation after another. They took over the governments of the countries and forced the German rule upon the people.

At that time, Italy and Japan were also ruled by dictators. They, too, waged war against their unprepared neighbors. Finally the free peoples of the world became alarmed. They realized the dictators were trying

349

to "rule the world." Some of the democratic countries declared war against the dictators. Their soldiers fought bravely for the cause of freedom.

For a time the United States only helped the free countries. But on December 7, 1941, Japan attacked our warships anchored at Pearl Harbor, Hawaii. *She bombed them without warning!* The next day Congress and the President declared war upon Japan. Two days later Germany and Italy, the partners of Japan, declared war upon the United States. We now faced powerful enemies across the Atlantic and the Pacific.

The Second World War was the most terrible war in all history. Our soldiers fought in many parts of the world. Finally Germany and Italy were defeated, but Japan fought on.

In August, 1945, the United States dropped atom bombs on two Japanese cities. The cities were almost destroyed and thousands of people were killed or injured for life. Not long after this, Japan, too, surrendered.

The war was over — but it cost the world billions of dollars and millions of lives!

THE UNITED NATIONS

After the Second World War, men and women in many countries were weary, heartsick, and tired of war. "Is there not some way to keep our boys from being killed?" they asked. "Is there not some way to stop the terrible suffering and waste of war?"

In 1945 delegates from fifty countries met in San Francisco. They met to discuss two important questions: *How could the nations of the world unite to prevent war? How could they work together to help the peoples of the world find freedom and happiness?*

For many days the delegates discussed these questions. Then they wrote a *charter*, or a plan, for an organization of nations. They called the organization the *United Nations*. The United Nations tries to keep peace in the world and help nations that are in need. Sixty countries have already joined the organization.

The United Nations is made up of several sections, or agencies. The two most important are the General Assembly and the Security Council.

The *General Assembly* is composed of delegates from every nation that belongs to the organization. It meets once a year to talk over the problems of the world. The Assembly may suggest peaceful means of settling world problems, but it may not advise the use of force.

The *Security Council* is composed of five permanent members: the United States, Great Britain, France, Russia, and China. The Council has six other members, which are elected by the General Assembly. These members serve for a term of two years.

The purpose of the Security Council is to keep peace in the world. The Council is really designed as a "police force." If two nations have a dispute, the Council investigates the trouble and suggests peaceful ways of settling the quarrel. The Council may also suggest armed force if it believes this is necessary.

The Council has helped to solve a number of disputes in a peaceful manner. It has suggested force only once. When North Korean Communists invaded the country of South Korea, the United Nations ordered them to return home. When they did not do so, the Council sent United Nations forces to help the South Koreans.

For a while the North Koreans lost ground rapidly. Then Communists from China joined the North Koreans. After the Chinese Communists entered the conflict, there were many fierce battles between the Communist forces and the soldiers of the United Nations. Many men on both sides were killed or wounded, and there was much suffering.

But the United Nations is still trying to find a way to help Korea become a peaceful and happy nation. It is still looking for a way to avoid wars, so that all nations can live at peace with one another.

American soldiers have been called upon to fight in many parts of the world. But we can be thankful our leaders do not *seek* war. We can be grateful that they still believe everyone has the right to "life, liberty, and the pursuit of happiness."

KEEP AMERICA A GOOD PLACE TO LIVE

The country you know is a good place to live. It has a pleasant climate and beautiful scenery. It is rich in *natural resources*. A natural resource is something given to us by nature. Minerals, forests, water, fertile soil, coal, oil, wild game, and fish are all gifts of nature.

When the early settlers came to America, they found a land rich in natural resources. Great forests covered much of the land. Rich stores of minerals were hidden in the mountains. The soil in the valleys was fertile. The prairies were covered with grassy meadows. Wild animals roamed through the forests. Fish and other sea food were plentiful.

Then the building of America began! Forests were cleared and homes were built. Highways, factories, towns, and cities took the place of the forests and the rich meadowlands. The settlers worked with a will, but they did not plan for the future.

The United States is still rich in natural resources. But there is a grave danger. Our supply of good coal is not so plentiful. There is not so much petroleum. There are not so many fish or fur-bearing animals as there once were. There are not so many valuable forests.

Our nation is not two hundred years old. *Yet almost one third of our country's known resources have been used.* Many of them have been wasted.

The early lumber companies used only the finest trees and destroyed the others. The early miners used only the best grades of ore and threw the rest away. The oil companies pumped oil faster than it could be used. Thoughtless hunters wiped out great herds of wild game, merely for the sport of it.

Such waste cannot continue. We must learn to plan, not only for today, but for tomorrow. We must learn to conserve the resources that nature has given us. *To conserve means to save and to use wisely.*

Everyone must take care of his own property. He must conserve the resources of the nation. The mother who does not waste food in the kitchen is being a good citizen. The father who takes care of his tools and keeps the house repaired is being a good citizen. A boy or a girl who takes care of his own property and the *property of others* is being a good citizen.

Take care of your clothes, your books, and your home. Take care of public property. Do not destroy our beautiful scenery. Do not leave campfires that will cause great forest fires. *Obey the laws.*

The explorers, the colonists, the pioneers, and all the Americans of yesterday have given you a good country. Be proud of it! *Make your country proud of you.* Keep America a good place to live!

Our country is rich in natural resources. In the forests and mountains are many fur-bearing animals. In the hills are rich metals.

Fertile soil is another of our resources. Many parts of our land have rich farms, green pastures, and fine fruit orchards.

There is water to irrigate the growing crops and to furnish water power to run busy factories. From the water we take many fish.

354

Oil wells dot many parts of the country. Oil pumped from them is worth millions of dollars. It is one of our rich resources.

Coal is another natural resource. It provides power for factories and heat for homes. Drugs and clothes are made from it.

Our great forests are valuable, too. *The United States has many, many resources that make our country a good place to live.*

THINGS TO DO

1. Make a chart entitled "Things That Make Our Country a Good Place to Live." Collect, or draw, pictures that will illustrate your chart.

2. Make a series of pictures showing some of the rights of "life, liberty, and the pursuit of happiness."

3. Make a chart entitled "How We Can Help to Keep Our Country a Good Place in Which to Live." Underneath the pictures you choose to illustrate your chart, write short sentences explaining them. You might also make your pictures into a frieze that can be placed along the top of your blackboard.

4. List the things you can do to be a good citizen at home, at school, and at play.

5. Find newspaper articles about the work of the United Nations. Put the articles on your class bulletin board.

LET'S TALK ABOUT—

1. The things that make our country a good place to live.

2. How schools and churches help to make our country a good place to live.

3. What you think "freedom of religion, freedom of speech, and freedom of the press" mean.

4. How you can help to keep our country a *free* country and a *good place to live.*

5. What you think Lincoln meant when he said, ". . . that government of the people, by the people, for the people, shall not perish from the earth."

6. The things described in the song "America the Beautiful" that make our country a good place to live.

AMERICA THE BEAUTIFUL

O beautiful for spacious skies,
For amber waves of grain,
For purple mountain majesties
Above the fruited plain.
America! America!
God shed His grace on thee,
And crown thy good with brotherhood
From sea to shining sea!

O beautiful for heroes proved
In liberating strife,
Who more than self their country loved
And mercy more than life.
America! America!
May God thy gold refine
Till all success be nobleness
And every gain divine.

O beautiful for patriot dream
That sees beyond the years
Thine alabaster cities gleam,
Undimmed by human tears.
America! America!
God shed His grace on thee,
And crown thy good with brotherhood
From sea to shining sea!

—*Katherine Lee Bates*

Toll was paid to provide better roads.

Transportation on early canals was slow.

Stagecoach travel was slow and tiresome.

Clipper ships speeded ocean transportation.

Automobiles brought better transportation.

Modern liners are like floating cities.

Modern travel is fast and comfortable.

Airplanes are swiftest form of travel.

Pony Express was once fast mail to the West.

Inventions make home life more pleasant.

Inventions improve modern communication.

Science helps modern fire fighters.

Invention of cotton gin developed industries.

Schools make America a better country.

Modern machinery makes farming easier.

America is rich in natural resources.

George Washington becomes our first president   1789
Spinning mills are built in New England
Eli Whitney invents the cotton gin
Settlers travel west by flatboats and covered wagons
The National Road from Maryland to Ohio is begun

Fulton demonstrates a successful steamboat   1807
Macadam roads are built

The Erie Canal is opened   1825
Successful steam locomotives are built
Cyrus McCormick invents a successful reaper
Horace Mann works for public schools
The telegraph is invented
Howe invents the sewing machine

Gold is discovered in California   1848
Clipper ships race around Cape Horn
The Pony Express carries the mail

Lincoln is elected president   1860

The first transcontinental railroad is completed   1869

Alexander Graham Bell invents the telephone   1876
The phonograph is invented
Edison invents a good electric light
The first automobiles are made

The wireless telegraph is invented   1896
Rural Free Delivery of mail is established

The Wright brothers successfully fly an airplane   1903
Motion pictures are shown in theaters
Electrical appliances are developed
Tractors are used on farms

World War I is fought   1914-1918
Radio programs are broadcast
A national system of highways is started
Lindbergh flies across the Atlantic

World War II is fought   1939-1945

The United Nations send armed forces to Korea   1950

INDEX

INDEX

A

Airplane, 304, 305
Alamo, 223, 224–25
Alaska, 268
America: Columbus discovers, 18, 19; naming of, 19; Vikings discover, 3
America, Central, 18, 42
America, South, 18, 42
America the Beautiful, 357
Appalachian Mountains, 175, 207, 212, 222
Armistice Day, 349
Atom bombs, 350
Austin, Stephen F., 226–27
Automobile, 291

B

Balboa, Vasco Núñez de, 27–29
Balloon, 304
Baltimore, Lord, 116–17
Bayberry candle, 146
Bell, Alexander Graham, 311
Betty lamp, 144
Bird Woman, 209–11
Blockhouse, 205
Book of Heaven, 230
Boone, Daniel, 204–07
Boonesboro, 205, 207
Boston, 101, 142, 180–83, 187
Boston Tea Party, 181–82

C

Cable: under Atlantic, 310; across Pacific, 311
Cabot, John, 64
California: becomes a state, 245; covered-wagon journey to, 233–37; discovery of gold in, 244–45
Calvert, Cecil, 116–17
Calvert, George, 116
Calvert, Leonard, 117
Camp meetings, 341
Canal: Chinese, 6; Erie, 299; Panama, 272–73
Canal Zone, 272
Candles: colonial, 145–46; pioneer, 215
Cape Cod Harbor, 96
Capital of the United States, 191
Caravan, 10, 233–36
Carolina, North, 124–25
Carolina, South, 124–25
Carriages, colonial, 290
Cartier, Jacques, 53
Carts, colonial, 290
Central America, 18, 42
Champlain, Samuel de, 56–57
Chariots, colonial, 290
Charlestown, 124, 181
Charter, United Nations, 351
Chesapeake Bay, 117
China, 6–7, 11

363

F

Factories: bring cities, 332; in early America, 317, 332; in England, 317; later colonial, 319, 332; today, 332
Farewell Address, Washington's, 191
Farming: early colonial, 89, 97, 117, 124–25, 169; early French, 87; early Spanish, 84; pioneer, 245, 322, 323; today, 323
Farming tools, early, 322
Farming tools, modern, 323
Ferdinand, King, 16
Field, Cyrus W., 310
Fire departments: colonial, 333; today, 333
Flag, 187
Flag Day, 187
Flatboat, 213, 298
Flax, 147
Florida, 39, 42, 43, 83
Foods: colonial, 144, 167; pioneer, 212, 214, 215; today, 329
Foot stoves, 157
Fort Sumter, 253
Forty-niners, 244–45, 300
France, help from, for colonists, 188
Franklin, Benjamin, 180, 189
French and Indian Wars: end of, 176–77; events leading to, 175–76
French explorers: Cartier, 53, 57; Champlain, 56–57; Jolliet, 60–61; La Salle, 61; Marquette, 60–61
French settlers, 86–87
Frontier, 202
Fulton, Robert, 299–300
Furniture: Dutch, 166; early colonial, 141; later colonial, 169; pioneer, 215; plantation, 164

G

Gadsden Purchase, 227
Gage, General, 182

General Assembly, United Nations, 351
George III, King, 181–82, 186
Georgia, 132–33
Gettysburg, 339
Gliders, 304–05
Gold, discovery of, 244
Gold rush, 244
Golden Hind, 67
Gorges, Sir Ferdinando, 128
Grant, Ulysses S., 254–55
Great Plains: homes on, 261–62; schools on, 263; settling of, 260–61
Greenland, 3, 64
Guam, 269

H

Habitants, 87
Hacienda, 84
Hackles, 147
Half Moon, 70
Hartford, beginning of, 109
Hawaiian Islands, 268–69
Henry, Prince, 11
Hitler, 349
Homes: colonial, 142; dugout, 142; later colonial, 169; in Middle Colonies, 165–66; Mormon, 241; Pilgrim, 140–41; pioneer, 205, 214; plantation, 162, 163, 164; prairie, 261–62; wigwam, 142
Homestead Act, 261, 264
Hooker, Thomas, 108–09
Hornbook, 156
House-raising, 160, 214
Houston, General Sam, 224–26, 227
Howe, Elias, 326
Hudson: Bay, 71; River, 71; Strait, 71
Hudson, Henry, 70–71

I

Iceland, 3

365

Polk, President, 227
Police departments: colonial, 333; to-
day, 333
Polo, Marco, 6–7, 10
Ponce de León, 39
Pony express, 308–09
Portugal, 11, 15
Potomac River, 117, 190, 191
Power looms, 317, 319
Prairie: homes, 261–62; schools, 263
Preacher, circuit, 341
Promontory Point, 295
Provincetown, 96
Puerto Rico, 39, 269
Puncheon, 214, 215
Punishment, colonial, 101, 158–59
Puritans, 100–01, 104–05
Pursuit of happiness, 345

Q

Quaker, 121, 165, 168
Quebec, 53, 57, 176, 177
Quilting bee, 161

R

Radio, 311
Railroad, transcontinental, 295
Rancheros, 84
Ranchers on plains, 260–61
Reaper, 322–23
Republic, 339
Reservations, Indian, 265
Resources, natural: conservation of,
353; destruction of, 353; kinds of,
352
Revere, Paul, 183
Rhode Island, 105
Roads: colonial, 285; concrete, 287;
corduroy, 287; hard-surface, 286;
macadam, 286
Ross, Betsy, 187
Russians, 268

S

Sacajawea, 209–11, 230
St. Augustine, 83
St. Lawrence, 53, 56
Salt Lake Valley, 240–41
Samoset, 97
San Jacinto River, 225
San Salvador, 18
Santa Anna, 223, 225
Santa Fe, 83
Santa Fe Trail, 232
Santa María, 16
Schoolhouses: colonial, 155; prairie,
263
Schools: colonial, 154–56; in Middle
Colonies, 167, 168; prairie, 263; in
Southern Colonies, 164; today, 340–
41
Security Council, United Nations, 351
Settlers, first: English, 88–89; French,
86–87; Spanish, 83–85
Settlers, western: clothes of, 215–16;
government helps, 203, 208; homes
of, 214, 215; pathfinders help, 204;
at play, 216–17; treaties help, 207,
227, 232; work of, 205, 214, 215–
16, 241, 244–45, 261, 262
Sewing machine, 326
Sierra Nevada, 237
Slater, Samuel, 317, 318
Smith, John, 88–89
Snake River, 211
Soapmaking, colonial, 145
South America, 18, 42
South Carolina, 124–25
South Sea, 29
Spanish explorers: Balboa, 27–29;
Columbus, 15–19; Coronado, 46–
47; De Soto, 42–43; Magellan, 32–
33; Ponce de León, 39
Spanish settlers, 83–85
Spike, golden, 295
Spinning, 147, 151

368